MABON

Llewellyn's Sabbat Essentials

MABON

Rituals, Recipes & Lore for the Autumn Equinox

Llewellyn Publications
Woodbury, Minnesota

FIRST EDITION
Tenth Printing, 2020

Book design: Donna Burch-Brown
Cover art: iStockphoto.com/18232461/©lectric_Crayon,
        iStockphoto.com/20924946/©Andrew_Howe,
        iStockphoto.com/17216777/©tatarnikova,
        iStockphoto.com/4402945/©LICreate
Cover design: Kevin R. Brown
Interior illustrations: Mickie Mueller

Llewellyn Publications is a registered trademark of Llewellyn Worldwide Ltd.

Library of Congress Cataloging-in-Publication Data
Rajchel, Diana.
  Mabon : rituals, recipes, and lore for the autumn equinox. -- First Edition.
    pages cm. -- (Llewellyn's sabbat essentials ; #5)
  Includes bibliographical references and index.
  ISBN 978-0-7387-4180-2
1. Mabon. 2. Witchcraft. I. Title.
  BF1572.M33R35 2015
  299'.94--dc23
                        2014044405

Llewellyn Publications
A Division of Llewellyn Worldwide Ltd.
2143 Wooddale Drive
Woodbury, MN 55125-2989
www.llewellyn.com

Printed in the United States of America

Contents

in resin - purification, prosperity, the mysteries of witchcraft,
ancestors, echinacea - healing, strengthening hyssop - purifica
tection, patience, loyalty, eternal life, concentration, love myrrh
- purification, protection, spirituality, Solomon's seal - exor
ing, purification, connecting to ancestors, connecting to land y
ak - protection, luck, health, money, fertility. Pine - healing
- protection, prosperity, health, the sea Maple - love, friend
sm prosperity, healing, prosperity, sleep Flowers carnation
marigold - protection, healing sunflower - purity, optimism
re no stones specifically associated with Mabon. However, so
s or sun dials are appropriate to this holiday. Animals, tote
uiding animals in the Mabinogion that helped lead Arthur's
irit world the Blackbird - one of the guiding animals in the
sperity, men to Mabon; brings messages of other worlds to te
of the guiding animals in the Mabinogion that helped lead
hunting and wisdom the Eagle - one of the guiding animals
land Arthur's men to Mabon; associated with wisdom, insig
almon - one of the guiding animals in the Mabinogion that
alon of knowledge and past and future the Goose - geese we

LLEWELLYN'S
SABBAT
ESSENTIALS

*L*LEWELLYN'S SABBAT ESSENTIALS provides instruction and inspiration for honoring each of the modern witch's sabbats. Packed with spells, rituals, meditations, history, lore, invocations, divination, recipes, crafts, and more, each book in this eight-volume series explores both the old and new ways of celebrating the seasonal rites that act as cornerstones in the witch's year.

There are eight sabbats, or holidays, celebrated by Wiccans and many other Neopagans (modern Pagans) today. Together, these eight sacred days make up what's known as the Wheel of the Year, or the sabbat cycle, with each sabbat corresponding to an important turning point in nature's annual journey through the seasons.

Devoting our attention to the Wheel of the Year allows us to better attune ourselves to the energetic cycles of nature and listen to what each season is whispering (or shouting!) to us, rather than working against the natural tides. What better time to start new projects than as the earth reawakens after a long winter, and suddenly everything is blooming and growing and shooting up out of the ground again? And what better time to meditate and plan ahead than during the introspective slumber of winter? With Llewellyn's Sabbat Essentials, you'll learn how to focus on the spiritual aspects of the Wheel of the Year, how to move through it and with it in harmony, and how to celebrate your own ongoing growth and achievements. This may be your first book on Wicca, Witchcraft, or Paganism, or your newest addition to a bookcase or e-reader already crammed with magickal wisdom. In either case, we hope you will find something of value here to take with you on your journey.

Take a Trip Through the Wheel of the Year

The eight sabbats each mark an important point in nature's annual cycles. They are depicted as eight evenly spaced spokes on a wheel representing the year as a whole; the dates on which they fall are nearly evenly spaced on the calendar, as well.

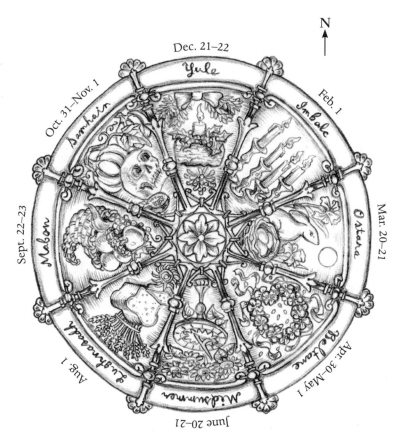

Wheel of the Year—Northern Hemisphere
(All solstice and equinox dates are approximate,
and one should consult an almanac or a calendar
to find the correct dates each year.)

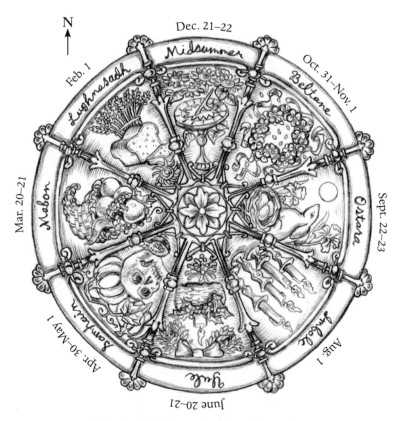

N ↑

Dec. 21–22

Feb. 1

Midsummer

Lughnasadh

Oct. 31–Nov. 1

Beltane

Mar. 20–21

Mabon

Ostara

Sept. 22–23

Apr. 30–May 1

Samhain

Imbolc

Aug. 1

Yule

June 20–21

Wheel of the Year—Southern Hemisphere

The Wheel is comprised of two groups of four holidays each. There are four solar festivals relating to the sun's position in the sky, dividing the year into quarters: the Spring Equinox, the Summer Solstice, the Fall Equinox, and the Winter Solstice, all of which are dated astronomically and thus vary slightly from year to year. Falling in between these quarter days are the cross-quarter holidays, or fire festivals: Imbolc, Beltane, Lughnasadh, and Samhain. The quarters are sometimes called the Lesser Sabbats and the cross-quarters the Greater Sabbats, although neither cycle is "superior" to the other. In the Southern Hemisphere, seasons are opposite those in the north, and the sabbats are consequently celebrated at different times.

While the book you are holding only focuses on Mabon, it can be helpful to know how it fits in with the cycle as a whole.

The Winter Solstice, also called Yule or Midwinter, occurs when nighttime has reached its maximum length; after the solstice, the length of the days will begin to increase. Though the cold darkness is upon us, there is a promise of brighter days to come. In Wiccan lore, this is the time when the young solar god is born. In some Neopagan traditions, this is when the Holly King is destined to lose the battle to his lighter aspect, the Oak King. Candles are lit, feasts are enjoyed, and evergreen foliage is brought in the house as a reminder that, despite the harshness of winter, light and life have endured.

At Imbolc (also spelled Imbolg), the ground is just starting to thaw, signaling that it's time to start preparing the fields for the approaching sowing season. We begin to awaken from our months of introspection and start to sort out what we have learned over that time, while also taking the first steps to make plans for our future. Some Wiccans also bless candles at Imbolc, another symbolic way of coaxing along the now perceptibly stronger light.

On the Spring Equinox, also known as Ostara, night and day are again equal in length, and following this, the days will grow longer than the nights. The Spring Equinox is a time of renewal, a time to plant seeds as the earth once again comes to life. We decorate eggs as a symbol of hope, life, and fertility, and we perform rituals to energize ourselves so that we can find the power and passion to live and grow.

In agricultural societies, Beltane marked the start of the summer season. Livestock were led out to graze in abundant pastures and trees burst into beautiful and fragrant blossom. Rituals were performed to protect crops, livestock, and people. Fires were lit and offerings were made in the hopes of gaining divine protection. In Wiccan mythos, the young god impregnates the young goddess. We all have something we want to harvest by the end of the year—plans we are determined to realize—and Beltane is a great time to enthusiastically get that process in full swing.

The Summer Solstice is the longest day of the year. It's also called Litha, or Midsummer. Solar energies are at their apex, and the power of nature is at its height. In Wiccan lore, it's the time when the solar god's power is at its greatest (so, paradoxically, his power must now start to decrease), having impregnated the maiden goddess, who then transforms into the earth mother.

In some Neopagan traditions, this is when the Holly King once again battles his lighter aspect, this time vanquishing the Oak King. It's generally a time of great merriment and celebration.

At Lughnasadh, the major harvest of the summer has ripened. Celebrations are held, games are played, gratitude is expressed, and feasts are enjoyed. Also known as Lammas, this is the time we celebrate the first harvest—whether that means the first of our garden crops or the first of our plans that have come to fruition. To celebrate the grain harvest, bread is often baked on this day.

The Autumn Equinox, also called Mabon, marks another important seasonal change and a second harvest. The sun shines equally on both hemispheres, and the lengths of night and day are equal. After this point, the nights will again be longer than the days. In connection with the harvest, the day is celebrated as a festival of sacrifice and of the dying god, and tribute is paid to the sun and the fertile earth.

To the Celtic people, Samhain marked the start of the winter season. It was the time when the livestock was slaughtered and the final harvest was gathered before the inevitable plunge into the depths of winter's darkness. Fires were lit to help wandering spirits on their way, and offerings were given in the names of the gods and the ancestors. Seen as a beginning, Samhain is now often called the Witches' New Year. We honor our ancestors, wind down our activities, and get ready for the months of introspection ahead ... and the cycle continues.

The Modern Pagan's Relationship to the Wheel

Modern Pagans take inspiration from many pre-Christian spiritual traditions, exemplified by the Wheel of the Year. The cycle of eight festivals we recognize throughout modern Pagandom today was never celebrated in full by any one particular pre-Christian culture. In the 1940s and 1950s, a British man named Gerald Gardner created the new religion of Wicca by drawing on a variety of cultures and traditions, deriving and adapting practices from pre-Christian religion, animistic beliefs, folk magick, and various shamanic disciplines and esoteric orders. He combined multicultural equinox and solstice traditions with Celtic feast days and early European agricultural and pastoral celebrations to create a single model that became the framework for the Wiccan ritual year.

This Wiccan ritual year is popularly followed by Wiccans and witches, as well as many eclectic Pagans of various stripes. Some Pagans only observe half of the sabbats, either the quarters or the cross-quarters. Other Pagans reject the Wheel of the Year altogether and follow a festival calendar based on the culture of whatever specific path they follow rather than a nature-based agrarian cycle. We all have such unique paths in Paganism that it is important not to make any assumptions about another's based on your own; maintaining an open and positive attitude is what makes the Pagan community thrive.

Many Pagans localize the Wheel of the Year to their own environment. Wicca has grown to become a truly global religion, but few of us live in a climate mirroring Wicca's British Isles origins. While traditionally Imbolc is the beginning of the thaw and the awakening of the earth, it is the height of winter in many northern climes. While Lammas may be a grateful celebration of the harvest for some, in areas prone to drought and forest fires it is a dangerous and uncertain time of year.

There are also the two hemispheres to consider. While it's winter in the Northern Hemisphere, it's summer in the Southern Hemisphere. While Pagans in America are celebrating Yule and the Winter Solstice, Pagans in Australia are celebrating Midsummer. The practitioner's own lived experiences are more important than any dogma written in a book when it comes to observing the sabbats.

In that spirit, you may wish to delay or move up celebrations so that the seasonal correspondences better fit your own locale, or you may emphasize different themes for each sabbat as you experience it. This series should make such options easily accessible to you.

No matter what kind of place you live on the globe, be it urban, rural, or suburban, you can adapt sabbat traditions and practices to suit your own life and environment. Nature is all around us; no matter how hard we humans try to insulate ourselves from nature's cycles, these recurring seasonal changes are inescapable. Instead of swimming against the tide, many modern Pagans embrace each season's unique energies, whether dark, light, or in between, and integrate these energies into aspects of our own everyday lives.

Llewellyn's Sabbat Essentials series offers all the information you need in order to do just that. Each book will resemble the one you hold in your hands. The first chapter, *Old Ways*, shares the history and lore that have been passed down, from mythology and pre-Christian traditions to any vestiges still seen in modern life. *New Ways* then spins those themes and elements into the manners in which modern Pagans observe and celebrate the sabbat. The next chapter focuses on *Spells and Divination* appropriate to the season or based in folklore, while the following one, *Recipes and Crafts*, offers ideas for decorating your home, hands-on crafts, and recipes that take advantage of seasonal offerings. The chapter *Prayers and Invocations* provides ready-made calls and prayers you may use in ritual, meditation, or journaling. The *Rituals of Celebration* chapter provides three complete rituals: one for a solitary, one for two people, and one for a whole group such as a coven, circle, or grove. (Feel free to adapt each or any ritual to your own needs, substituting your own offerings, calls, invocations, magickal workings, and so on. When planning a group ritual, try to be conscious of any special needs participants may have. There are many wonderful books available that delve into the fine points of facilitating ritual if you don't have experience in this department.) Finally, in the back of the book you'll find a complete list of correspondences for the holiday, from magickal themes to deities to foods, colors, symbols, and more.

By the end of this book you'll have the knowledge and the inspiration to celebrate the sabbat with gusto. By honoring the Wheel of the Year, we reaffirm our connection to nature so that as her endless cycles turn, we're able to go with the flow and enjoy the ride.

OLD WAYS

... resin - purification, prosperity, the mysteries of autumn eg... ancestors, echinacea - healing, strengthening hyssop - purifica... tion, patience, loyalty, eternal life, concentration, love myrrh... purification, protection, spirituality, Solomon's seal - exorc... ng, purification, connecting to ancestors, connecting to land y... k - protection, luck, health, money, fertility. Pine - healing... - protection, prosperity, health, the sea Maple - love, friend... ... prosperity, healing, prosperity, sleep Flowers carnation... marigold - protection, healing sunflower - purity, optimism... ... no stones specifically associated with Mabon. However, sto... ... or sun dials are appropriate to this holiday. Animals, tote... ...ding animals in the Mabinogion that helped lead Arthur's... ...it world the Blackbird - one of the guiding animals in the... ...perity, men to Mabon; brings messages of other worlds to the... ... of the guiding animals in the Mabinogion that helped lead... ...hunting and wisdom the Eagle - one of the guiding animals... ...and Arthur's men to Mabon; associated with wisdom, insig... ...lmon - one of the guiding animals in the Mabinogion that... ...dom of knowledge and past and future the Goose - asso...

$\mathcal{H}$ARVEST FESTIVALS CELEBRATED more than finished work for the season; they celebrated the capacity to survive the winter. The best known of these harvest festivals was the Eleusinian Mysteries, a weeklong celebration in ancient Greece that fell close to the Autumn Equinox. Mabon is a modern addition to these celebrations of harvest, sacrifice, and survival. While Wiccans often think of Mabon as "Pagan Thanksgiving," those who recognize the dying god myths inherent to the holiday may also acknowledge it as a sort of "Pagan Easter." Mabon gives thanks not just for our food, but for the sacrifices necessary for us to survive.

Sabbat celebrations mark seasonal points most familiar to the British worldview, with equinoxes happening in September and March and solstices occurring in June and December. For Pagans outside the Northern Hemisphere, most assume the perspective that a nature religion must honor nature as it is and shift their practices to suit their own locations. Not everyone lives where it snows, where it rains frequently, or where summer might indeed end at that certain point around

Samhain. Perhaps the orange trees stop bearing fruit or different vegetables ripen. Perhaps the sea becomes choppy. Colder weather requires wearing a sweater in the morning, only to shed it later, instead of donning a coat and boots.

An equinox happens when the plane of Earth's equator passes the center of the sun. This occurs twice a year: at the Spring Equinox and at the Fall Equinox. This results in the Northern and Southern Hemispheres of the earth experiencing equal illumination. For those who live close to the equator, an equinox is one of only two times of year that the sun is at a subsolar point—the point where the center of the sun, when it hits its zenith, is directly overhead.

When this happens in March, the Northern Hemisphere receives increasing light day by day (while the Southern Hemisphere sees it decrease). In September, the halves of the earth trade their light. The extremes of this trade are less dramatic for those who live close to the equator and increases in extremism farther away from it. Latitudes located halfway between the equator and the North or South Poles experience a day with even—or close to even—distribution between light and dark.

This distribution and the complications that make every harvest unpredictable are why Mabon is often celebrated within a range of days rather than specifically on the traditional dates of September 20 or 21. The equinox is not just a one-day event. It can happen over a span of two to three days depending on the location. Since Fall Equinox traditions center on the work of the harvest, allowing a few days to acknowledge the shifting light makes sense. Few farmers or gardeners can haul in all their new growth over the course of a single day. Harvesting is a process that takes weeks, sometimes months. The work of gathering begets the work of winnowing, stacking, pickling, baking, and preserving. As the light wanes, the urgency of the work increases.

Astrology of Fall Equinox

Astrology does more than define personalities; it also marks seasons and, to some degree, can imply actions appropriate to a season. In the case of Mabon, the Autumn Equinox happens as the sun enters the sign of Libra. Libra, represented by the scales, is uniquely appropriate. The sign that represents level-headed balance and careful judgment is the most necessary outlook to have when preparing for a rougher season to come. Harvest requires decisions about what to store and what to consume. What should we leave to decay in the fields? What bulbs should we plant in the ground to await the force of the Spring Equinox? What can we safely do without through the winter?

For those who plan their lives according to astrological precepts, Libra and the Autumn Equinox mark a time to harvest what you have grown in the past year and a time to take an honest look at what you need to let go. You need not drop everything right away—operating on these astrological and seasonal cycles does give you some time for a gentle separation. You can also use the coming of the sign as a time to take precautions. Start a savings plan. Get your flu shots. Put that lock on your credit report.

We're Like Our Ancestors

We are not as distant from our ancestors as we might like to think. We still depend on food grown somewhere—whether by our hands or the hands of a farmer—and we are still subject to seasonal changes, variable weather conditions, and environmental concerns that directly impact the way we live our daily lives. Technological advancement has yet to change our core dependence on agriculture.

We touch the same things our ancestors touched—the earth, the waters, and the air itself. While we often describe ourselves as being half from one parent and half from the other, the truth is far more complex. We are half a composite of our mother's ancestors and half a composite of our father's. We are not mere deposits from the generation before. We are the complex result of history. Even the most humble life has an ancient heritage attached, expressed as the DNA helix wraps and relinks to propose a new being, a new take on all that has come before.

Some need not look further into spiritual machinations to see that the ancestors are still with us. Others feel a need to add more to the story, more to explain our connections and interactions. Ancient myths served the purpose of offering explanations. All myths spoke to some deep truth that the dressings of fiction made easier to deliver. Pagans often draw from these myths to aid their own spiritual understanding of the universe. Some of those myths are memories of our ancestors, drawn broad, and aligned with nature itself. Others stories, such as the tales of Isis and Osiris or Demeter and Persephone, are filled with love, loss, planning to survive, and the other inevitabilities of life that we experience to this day.

Aidan Kelly and Mabon

It is Aidan Kelly, by his own account, who christened the modern Pagan Autumn Equinox celebration as *Mabon*. Before this, practitioners of Pagan religions simply called this seasonal holiday the Fall or Autumnal Equinox. The early Wiccans celebrated major fire festivals with the quarter sabbats observed at the nearest full moon. When Kelly initiated into Wicca, sabbat celebrations involved a ritual followed by a feast during each of the four major fire festivals (Imbolc, Beltane, Lughnasadh, and Samhain). Since the four fire festivals had Celtic names, Kelly attempted to balance them with Saxon names for the solar quarter festivals of equinoxes and solstices. Unfortunately, he could not find an ancient Saxon holiday name that quite fit the themes of the Wiccan Autumn Equinox.

Kelly did find that the Eleusinian Mysteries fit the emotional role desired, but he did not want to throw a Greek name into the already established Celtic-Saxon scheme. Since he could not find a Saxon name, he resorted to neighboring Celtic sources. Kelly looked to the tale of Mabon ap Modron, the name meaning "son of the mother," for what he saw as a thematic parallel to Kore, which meant "daughter of the mother." He saw a spiritual link in the quintessential mother goddess having her child stolen. While Kelly drew spiritual inspiration for the holiday from the Eleusinian Mysteries, he used the name *Mabon* from the Celts for at least partial naming consistency in the sabbats.

Briefly, the tale of Mabon is that of an infant child stolen away from his mother and imprisoned. His release becomes the object of the mythic hero Culhwch, who must seek out Mabon to help him hunt down a wild boar that was previously a king in order to win the hand of Olwen in marriage. As Kelly suggested, there are parallels to the Persephone myth: "Mabon can be seen as a character who epitomizes the pan-European concept of the infant in exile and return. [...] This myth is indicative of the separation of the youthful god from his mother, the great goddess, and the resulting desolation of the land, which is only restored once the youthful god is re-united with his mother" (Hughes, 73).

In the Book of Taliesin, Mabon takes on a psychopompic aspect and was called on for those qualities, again making him an excellent representative of the Fall Equinox: "Here Mapo-nos is perceived as a god who traverses the fickle line between the under- and upperworld, the realm of light and darkness; having access to both worlds, he is useful to those who require the qualities of either state. Fertility, birth, and death, in the case of Mabon, are simply opposite sides of the same coin; all are necessary" (Hughes, 74).

Although the literature does not directly connect Mabon to the equinox, Kelly believes that the Celts did celebrate some holiday during the Autumn Equinox, mentioning that astrono-mer Sir Fred Hoyle determined this by examining Stonehenge. Hoyle discovered that a series of holes called Aubrey Holes lined up with specific eclipses, allowing light to show through at exactly the moment of equinox. Since Stonehenge appeared to serve as a predictive calendar, and it definitely aligned on the dates of equinoxes and solstices, Hoyle's discovery sup-ported Kelly's belief that there was some cultural significance of the dates to ancient Pagans in the British Isles as well.

While the Celtic heroic mythos is by and far the most popu-lar core to Wiccan celebrations, sabbats have definite spiritual themes but are not required to assume the tales of a specific culture as liturgy. The Mabon celebration gives thanks for the harvest and for sacrifices made by others to ensure survival. Several myths in many cultures share such themes.

The Eleusinian Mysteries

As mentioned previously, the Eleusinian Mysteries were a sacred harvest festival in ancient Greece. While archaeologists and historians have successfully pieced together some of the practices from the festival, much remains a mystery, including why so many parts of the celebration remained secret. The influence of these Mysteries spread across Europe; more than one scholar has speculated that later Pagan harvest traditions have roots in Eleusis.

The foundation of the Mysteries was the story of Demeter and Persephone/Kore. In this tale, Pluto fell in love with Kore and kidnapped her from the fields where she played, taking her back to his kingdom in Hades. When Demeter discovered her child missing, she searched everywhere on Earth for her. When at last she received word that Pluto was keeping her child, Demeter refused to let anything on Earth grow. Zeus, realizing that all his people would starve and die, was going to relent and insist Pluto release Persephone. Unfortunately, Persephone consumed six seeds from a pomegranate during her stay in the underworld. Because she had partaken the food of the dead, she became part of that kingdom, and according the laws of nature could not ascend to the world of the living. Demeter held firm, refusing to let anything else grow, and so Zeus, with the help of his messenger Hermes, negotiated a partial release so that Kore could come to the land every spring and return at autumn to rule the dead beside her husband.

While no one knows all of the events that conspired at the festival of the Eleusinian Mysteries, scholars have fragments of information about the practices, and they know that ancient Greeks took it very seriously. The festival of the Greater Mysteries happened once every four years in Eleusis and lasted nine or ten days. It always began at the full moon before the Autumn Equinox and included a procession. During this procession, farmers carried a holy basket in a consecrated cart while shouting "Hail Demeter!" It is conjectured that the festival participants sacrificed a pregnant sow to Demeter.

According to Aidan Kelly, at the climax, someone placed a mildly sedated little boy on a swing and pushed him across a giant bonfire; the swing then returned with a ram in the boy's place. At some point, a gong would sound and the priestess of Persephone appeared. Many of the known symbols of the Eleusinian Mystery tradition, such as grain and seeds, are also symbols in modern Pagan harvest and Mystery traditions.

The Dying God

The Golden Bough by James Frazer, a seminal anthropological work from the late nineteenth century, influenced spiritualist movements throughout the twentieth century that in turn influenced the development of modern Paganism. Much of what the author posited became the groundwork for the modern magickal-religious thought, especially passages now associated with Mabon.

Frazer's research on the Divine King motif fits with many of its motifs as they relate to harvest, death, and sacrifice. Many Pagans find meaning in the harvest and death myths that parallel across cultures. Dionysus, the god of wine and the keeper of the mysteries of the grape, died when his mother, pregnant with him, died, and he was rescued at the last moment by his father Zeus. Adonis, Aphrodite's lover, died when he angered Artemis during a hunt. These are all gods struck down as an allegory for the harvest cycle.

In these myths, each of these gods resurrects seasonally either as themselves or as a new form that originated in the god at the beginning of the story. Christo-Wiccans may identify this death and resurrection harvest theme with the death and resurrection of Jesus Christ. Some may also recognize parallels between Christ, the dying god mythology, and the Babylonian god Tammuz. Tammuz, mentioned in the Bible, endures a path that bears striking parallels to both the harvest god myths and the tales of Jesus Christ. Tammuz died in the fields of Babylon, had women weeping at his grave as Christ did, and later resurrected. These similarities suggest spiritual motifs that relate to Christian Easter. Christianity itself also had Mystery traditions around the life and death of Christ, as Pagans ancient and modern have Mystery traditions around life and death itself.

Greek Mystery traditions conveyed the secrets of cultivation and the connection between food and mortality. Frazer says of these mystery practices:

> They still thought that by performing certain magical rites they could aid the god who was the principle of life, in his struggle with the opposing principle of death. They imagined that they could recruit his failing energies and even raise him from the dead.

On a more subtle level, the spiritual themes of Mabon also highlighted the sacrifices of leadership. Every year, a leadership figure—the god—had to die to ensure the survival of his people. Since the dying god represented the god of vegetation, this usually was interpreted at the most basic level of survival. In the story of Isis and Osiris, the tale went beyond literal survival to a metaphorical survival when Osiris was torn apart by his enemy, Set, and then only resurrected after Isis and those loyal to her pieced together his body. Without Osiris, the land did not provide food. His energy as the god of vegetation was missing, as was his leadership, which kept people buoyed during hard seasons. This leadership theme also appeared in the tale of King Arthur, in the tale of Dionysus, and in the tale of Jesus Christ. In each story, the god figure sacrificed himself to the land for his people.

Mabon is, because of this inevitability of death association, a season of harvest and grief. Part of healing that grief is having a leader who can provide a morale boost to the people. With the god of the land gone, that leadership then falls to the goddess of the land. As the people lay the dying god to rest, the process that leads to the descent of the goddess at Samhain begins. The ancient Greek sang songs of mourning while they reaped, in Egypt the reaper cut the first few sheaves before pausing to beat his breast in mourning, and in Germany farmers often associated harvest time with death. Preindustrial European farmers still enacted some of these grief rituals in their farming.

Ritual Scapegoats

The designation of a ritual scapegoat was a common practice in the ancient world. This practice, where a person or an animal assumed the "sins" of the populous, represented the dying god sacrificing his life for the land and its people. While it did not always happen at the Autumn Equinox, the spiritual themes connect on a deep level to the modern sabbat. During Thargelia, a harvest celebration dedicated to Apollo, the community led a criminal through the city. At the outskirts of town, they then flogged this person. Sometimes the town leaders executed the criminal; at other times, they banished him from the city. This ritual symbolized an act of purification for the entire community. A criminal's removal meant the town's purification. As winter neared, some villages literally drove a goat through the town and then out of it, killing it at the outskirts to cleanse the community of all evil. Driving out the criminal or goat represented the practice of driving vermin from the crops. Ancient Greek farmers sacrificed wild pigs as a means of keeping pests —the pigs!—out of the crops.

While scapegoating is not a deliberate Pagan ritual practice, the symbolism of a sacrificed person and of pests driven out parallels the spiritual meaning of Mabon. We see a masculine figure taking in a destructive force and then removing it to ensure the community's survival.

John Barleycorn

John Barleycorn is a British folk song that teaches—in a dark-humored way—the process of cereal grain harvest. Barleycorn himself symbolizes the harvested vegetation. He acts as a symbol of the dying god and the ritual scapegoat at the same time.

The ditty, in its solemn yet playful tone, speaks to the sacrificial nature of the harvest. It may mark the transition some societies took from actual to metaphorical scapegoat practice, when effigies became reasonable sacrifices in and of themselves. The refrain, "John Barleycorn must die," makes it clear that this character must give his life and blood to the land so that the land has something to give back come spring. This folk song makes a clear link between sacrifice—whether literal or symbolic—and the fertilization of the land.

Harvest Home

Harvest Home is the English name for the harvest festival that occurred near Fall Equinox throughout Europe. Some ancient Pagans also referred to this time as the Ingathering. Many of these traditions came from old Pagan fertility rituals; over time, the ruling church dedicated the rituals to Christian saints instead of the original Pagan gods.

Other elements of these harvest traditions have roots not only in Paganism, but in feudal traditions where the farm laborers were serfs with their lives tied to land they farmed from birth. Harvest was a labor-intensive season, possibly the hardest work of the year. Consequently, the festival was one of combined work and play, with a great deal of merriment used to offset the serious business of preparation for winter. Harvest Home was more than a festival for the reapers; entire villages decorated doors with wreaths, and villagers hung fruits of the harvest from arches throughout the town.

Rituals in the form of games were very much part of the reaping process, especially when collecting the last sheaves. These games addressed the reapers' belief in an immanent spirit that lived in the corn; some areas saw this spirit as benevolent and others feared it. In Bavaria, people believed the corn mother punished farmers for their sins with bad crops. In Germany, reapers would sometimes hit the crop with a flail (a chain attached to a stick) to "drive out the wolf," thus driving evil spirits out of the fields before the reaping. The collection of these sheaves often spoke to that culture's feelings about the spirit of the corn.

The Last Sheaf

Hosts of traditions surround collecting the last sheaf. Whether collecting it meant good luck or bad depended on the European culture of that reaper. Often, its collection became a game. In one game, called "crying the mare," reapers took turns throwing sickles at the last sheaves. The person who knocked the last one down gave a ritual cry of "I have her." The sheaf also often had a local nickname that paralleled animals ancient Pagans used in sacrificial offerings. The last sheaf might have been called the ox (Germany), the hare (France), the cat (northern Germany), or the bull (Czech Republic).

Some places called the last sheaf "the dead one." Sometimes, in an act reminiscent of scapegoat practices, an animal, such as a rooster, a mare, or a sheep, was set loose in the fields or hidden under the final cut sheaves. Sometimes the person who caught it kept it as a prize. In some places in Europe, the reapers and farmers butchered the animal on the fields and then served its meat at the end of harvest feast (Hastings, 521).

Corn Dollies

The word "corn" in Europe referred to all kinds of grain, not just the maize crop familiar to North America. Because of this, the term "corn dolly" meant a figure fashioned from grain—usually wheat, but rye, millet, oats, and even maize also suited the purpose. In the British Isles, it was most commonly called a "corn dolly" but it might also be called the "mell-sheaf," a "kern baby," an "ivy girl," or even a "carline." There is evidence that this tradition does not originate in Europe. The Rosicrucian Museum in San Jose, California, has a corn dolly archaeologists recovered from ancient Egypt.

These dolls were central to the end of harvest traditions. The figures were male or female depending on the traditions of the region; even the doll's projected age reflected how people viewed the crop spirit. People decorated these sheaves with ribbons, other harvest plants, and fruits. Sometimes dollies came from the first sheaf, cut ceremonially at the beginning of harvest, usually by a young girl dubbed the "Harvest Queen" or by the reaper elected Harvest Lord; other times they were made from the last sheaf cut. The people of some locales symbolically fed these dollies and often sat them in places of honor during feasts, retiring them to the farmer's home until the next year, when the farmer ceremonially burned them. On the Isle of Man, for example, laborers made an effigy from wheat, decorated it with ribbons, and paraded it through the fields. A girl, usually the youngest in the community, led the procession while carrying the effigy. In other places, the corn dolly was loaded onto a cart and followed musicians playing pipes and tabors; often those following the procession sang harvest songs or cheered as they wheeled through. "Hip hip hooray!" was a phrase in one common harvest cheer. Often the farmer kept the dolly on a hearth or in a barn until the next year.

The Business of the Harvest

Harvest time was when laborers negotiated their wages and rents with the landowners. At the beginning of the harvest, the farm laborers held a dinner called the Feast of the Ingathering. At this feast, they nominated one of their own as "lord of the harvest." This man acted as the representative of the workers to the Lord of the Manor, the landowner who paid them for their harvest work (Warren, 216).

The lord of the harvest enjoyed certain honors; he cut down the first plants and was the first to eat and drink at his electoral feast. Reapers also often elected a second in command to work with him, a man that held the joking title "harvest lady." The harvest lord negotiated wages for all the workers, and the harvest lady acted as the leader in the fields when the lord went to make those negotiations.

Reapers celebrated the election with ale and a drinking game. Someone handed the "lady" a drinking horn that he then passed to the "lord." After he made good wishes and drank, the lady took the horn and made a toast. Then the rest of the reapers imbibed. Every time a person drank out of order, he or she had to pay a fine. That money paid for a later (or continued) party at a nearby alehouse. This particular type of party, called a scotale, was for the express purpose of drinking ale. The church disapproved of this practice.

Harvest Home Feast

Harvest Home, the feast that happened after the reapers cut the last sheaf, had different names and nicknames around Great Britain. Some called it the Feast of the Ingathering, others a mell-supper, some just called it "horkey" or a "scotale"—the same as the reapers' electoral feast (Warren, 216). At this feast, landowners sat down with those who worked their land. This dinner concluded all wage negotiations for the year; this also made it a village celebration, since most of the villagers also worked the Lord of the Manor's land.

The supper itself had many local traditions around it, from what people ate to games and dancing after the meal. Usually the corn dolly sat in the center of the feast table (or presided over the feast, if the event was large). In England, two men sometimes dressed up as a black sow and pinched or pricked random guests at the feast. Other times, the head reaper exited the feast and came back dressed as "lord"; he then collected money from the other reapers so that they could again go to an alehouse for a harvest after-party. The games often included cock fighting, pig catching, and wrestling.

When the Christian Church became dominant in Europe, Harvest Home festivals kept their Pagan flavor but adopted Christian saint's names. So Harvest Home became three separate festivals that all converged near the Autumn Equinox: the Feast of the Nativity of Saint Mary (September 8), the Feast of Saint Michael (Michaelmas, September 29), and the feast of Saint Martin (Martinmas, November 11). Michaelmas retained the traditions with the closest relationship to Harvest Home.

Michaelmas

The first known Michaelmas celebration happened in 1011 (Gomme, 270). Named for the archangel Michael, September 29 became both a harvest festival and a time of taking stock, hiring help, and settling debts. The English called these days of financial settlement "quarter days" as they took place four times a year. Around Michaelmas, families decided which animals to keep through the winter and how many to sell or slaughter. Intended to replace Harvest Home, Michaelmas marked the point near the end of the reaping season and concluded with a dinner for landowners and tenants. These dinners gave landlords an opportunity to collect their seasonal rents.

Tenants of the sixteenth century presented landlords with a goose on Michaelmas, in addition to their quarter-day rent payments. Eating a roast goose became a key Michaelmas tradition that eventually moved to Christmas. Livestock at the time constituted rent, making the bills settled on this day especially significant since the results of the harvest might determine whether a family had a home during the cold season. A saying in the British Isles that betold the importance of this holiday was "Eat a goose on Michaelmas Day and want not for money all the year."

The Scottish served bannock at Michaelmas, a cake with a sconelike texture made from cereal grains and then cooked in a lambskin. In Ireland, some baked a ring into a pie that was eaten at Michaelmas dinner. The person who found the ring was to be married in the next year. The Irish also considered Michaelmas an excellent day for fishing—perhaps because it was the last good day to do so for the year!

After Protestantism spread through England, many churches replaced Michaelmas with Harvest Festival, a revamped Harvest Home.

The myths about gods that die and return highlight the spiritual connection between the Eleusinian Mysteries, Harvest Home, Michaelmas, and Mabon. The harvest must end with death—and survival needs a plan. The farmer nurtured, fed, and cultivated the grain, creating a bond of survival with the plant. When harvest time comes, that relationship ends. As the Wheel of the Year turns, so the end of Mabon marks the barest of the beginnings of winter and as each day of autumn fades all look toward the cold, wondering what else we will lose to the coming darkness.

NEW WAYS

in terms – purification, prosperity, the mysteries of autumn ... ancestors, echinacea – healing, strengthening hyssop – purifi... ...tection, patience, loyalty, eternal life, concentration, love myrrh ... – purification, protection, spirituality, Solomon's seal – exor... ...ing, purification, connecting to ancestors, connecting to land ... ...ak – protection, luck, health, money, fertility, Pine – heal... ... – protection, prosperity, health, the sea Maple – love, frien... ...m, prosperity, healing, prosperity, sleep Flowers carnation ... marigold – protection, healing sunflower – purity, optimism ... ...re no stones specifically associated with Mabon. However, s... ...s or sun dials are appropriate to this holiday. Animals, tot... ...iding animals in the Mabinogion that helped lead Arthur ... ...rit world the Blackbird – one of the guiding animals in th... ...sperity, men to Mabon; brings messages of other worlds, to t... ...– of the guiding animals in the Mabinogion that helped lead ... ...hunting and wisdom the Eagle – one of the guiding animals ... ...lead Arthur's men to Mabon; associated with wisdom, insi... ...almon – one of the guiding animals in the Mabinogion that ... ...lon of knowledge and past and future the Goose – goose, an...

*T*HE EQUINOX, WITH its trade of light for dark, stirs strong emotions of loss as the ease of summer passes. While the celebrations of the harvest and the equinox have changed among modern people, especially Pagans, the core meaning remains the same: life is precious, and we are lucky to sustain it.

Mabon, because of its spiritual underpinnings, also must acknowledge shared secular values in order to experience the full, rich scope of this spoke on the Wheel of the Year.

Other Pagan Autumn Celebrations

Some Pagan traditions celebrate Mabon, but others celebrate other holidays on the Autumn Equinox. Some, especially Celtic Reconstructionist faiths, only observe the four major fire festivals, (Samhain, Imbolc, Beltane, and Lughnasadh) and do not do anything specific for Mabon. Autumn is also the time of the largest pan-Pagan (meaning "all Pagans") celebration in the world: Pagan Pride.

At this event, Pagans around the world gather to host public rituals and run a food drive. Their purpose is to educate the public about Pagan religions and thus to reduce xenophobia. Each celebration differs just a little bit: some run it like a street fair, others like a small convention, and others just host a picnic and invite the public. Pagans that participate in Pagan Pride often see the event as a sort of community reunion and an opportunity to interact with those outside their immediate spiritual circles. The public is invited and is encouraged to talk to Pagans about their beliefs and practices.

Pagan Pride borrowed its name directly from the Gay Pride movement. Both movements celebrate individuals choosing openness about who they are rather than hiding to protect themselves from society's sensibilities. While no one knows exactly when the first Pagan Pride event happened, an official Pagan Pride Project grew out of Cecylena Dewr's work with the Pagan Awareness League in 1997. Dewr proposed three elements to the project: first, that in every location that could gather enough Pagans, they host an event with at least one ritual open to the public, Pagan and non-Pagan alike. Second, that the pride event runs a food drive in honor of Mabon and other Thanksgiving holidays of the autumn season and to serve as a reminder to Pagans of their responsibilities to city, state, and country. Third, that organizers invite the press so they could see some positive portrayals of Paganism outside of the Halloween season. In 1998, the world saw the first international Pagan Pride Project with seventeen communities in the United States and one community in Canada participating. It had a total attendance of around nine hundred people. In 2000, Pagan Pride gained coverage from the *New York Times*; held its first events in Rome, Great Britain, and Brazil; and donated 8,671 pounds of food (and several thousand dollars) to charity. By 2005, the Pagan Pride Project counted over forty thousand attendees globally. While Pagan Pride International has stopped tracking its data, the celebrations around Mabon continue every year.

Druidry

Modern Druids celebrate the Autumn Equinox, calling it *Alban Elfed*. *Alban Elfed* means "the Light of the Water." This is a time when Druids observe darkness consuming more time than the light. They honor the equinox as a time to thank the Mother (their concept of the feminine Divine) for her abundance as it manifests in the harvest.

Hellenic Pagans

Modern Hellenics (people devoted to reconstructing ancient Greek religion) celebrate *Boedromion*, which translates from Greek to "September." This starts at sunset on the first new moon of September and honors different gods of the harvest for the next nine days, reminiscent of the Eleusinian festival.

Each day, Hellenists make offerings and libations to these gods in gratitude for an abundant harvest.

Heathens

Heathens, people of Norse Pagan traditions, call the Autumn Equinox *Winter Finding*. On the equinox, they hold a blot, where they make offerings to the god Odin and others in his pantheon with ale and bread. After sharing a meal, everyone present passes a drinking horn and makes boasts, takes vows, or honors their ancestors when the horn comes to them.

Traditional Witchcraft

Traditional witches are those who practice the forms of Witchcraft prevalent in the United Kingdom before the advent of Gerald Gardner. Sometimes they call themselves practitioners of the Craft. Others identify as Hedge Witches or Hedge Walkers. These people use shamanic methods and deep connection with nature to practice magick and to sense the Divine. Most celebrate the turn of the seasons and the holidays as befits the region they live in. Those who live in temperate zones may well have their own private practices to acknowledge Autumn Equinox.

Neopagans

Neopagans are Pagans who see themselves as modern polytheists but prefer not to affiliate with an organized form such as Wicca. Often they celebrate Mabon as a day of personal balance, designing their own rituals or simply honoring the change in seasons through their daily living practices.

Eclectic Witchcraft

Eclectic witches are Neopagans who draw from multiple traditions and backgrounds to create their own practices. If Mabon as the Autumn Equinox speaks to them, they will practice it, often using rituals they have designed based on their own spiritual experience and association with the harvest season.

Celtic Pagans

Some Celtic Pagans also call the Autumn Equinox *Feast of Avalon*. Avalon translates to "land of apples" in modern English, and often the apple harvest happens about this time (Springwolf).

Stregheria

Italian Witchcraft calls the Autumn Equinox the *Equinozio di Autunno*. This minor festival honors the earth. In their own sabbat cycle (*treguenda*), the Lord of Light becomes the Lord of Shadows and the god Janus dies and departs for the underworld.

Modern Harvest Festivals

Many Harvest Festivals now are both secular and spiritual, celebrating heritage and community together. Fewer people farm now, and in some ways that enhances the mystery. We must now make an effort to appreciate food and to learn where it comes from, and cultivation comes from a spiritual calling.

Harvest Festival in the United Kingdom

The United Kingdom has replaced Harvest Home with Harvest Festival. This holiday takes place on the Sunday closest to the full moon before the Autumn Equinox. Congregants decorate the churches with cornucopias, wreaths, and baskets, and parishioners give thanks for the bounty. Local farmers bring baskets filled with produce that local priests bless. After services, church members distribute the baskets of food to impoverished community members. After services, the community often has a celebration for the whole town that includes old games from the Harvest Home celebration.

Dozynki

Dozynki is the living Polish tradition of Harvest Home. The Slavic Pagan and feudal roots remain beneath the Catholic veneer. At Dozynki in medieval times, the landowner hosted a feast to reward his laborers for their backbreaking work through the season.

In the twenty-first century, the Polish celebrate Dozynki anytime between mid-September and late October. Celebrations usually include a harvest festival mass, sometimes held outdoors, followed by a procession either by someone representing the old "Lord of the Manor" or by two women selected for their competence in harvest work. The church is decorated with harvest baskets and crafts made from the grain crops.

Singing and procession is an important part of Dozynki celebration; the girl deemed the best at harvesting leads this processional and wears garlands woven of grain and decorated with wildflowers, apples, and ash berries. The girl or woman presents the symbolic lords and ladies of the manor with the wreath on her head—and this person gives that wreath a place of honor in his or her home. The person representing the Lord of the Manor then shares a shot of vodka with the eldest male harvester, toasts the entire group, and invites them to a feast hosted on his/her land.

Erntedankenfest

Erntedankfest is a series of festivals that take place throughout rural Germany. Erntedanktag, like Harvest Home/Harvest

Festival, includes a church service that displays baskets of local harvest bounty that afterward go to the poor. After services, civic celebrations include processions, parades, and a mix of Pagan-rooted traditions ranging from effigies made of corn to decorated beasts of burden.

Oktoberfest

Oktoberfest has purely civic origins. Started on October 12, 1810, to celebrate the royal wedding of Prince Ludwig and Therese of Saxony-Hildburghausen, the sixteen-day celebration has lasted more than two hundred years. It has been moved to September for better weather and has become something of a worldwide celebration observed where beer is served.

In 1811, Germany added horse races to the festival to enhance awareness of regional agriculture. Now the Munich festival hosts beer stands, festival rides, and a thriving annual fairground trade. While perhaps not a conscious harvest festival, Oktoberfest certainly celebrates specific aspects of agriculture as Mabon in the Pagan context does.

Jewish Holidays in September

September is an especially sacred time for the Jewish faith, with each week marking a day of spiritual significance, many of which share similar spiritual meanings with Mabon. While ancient Jews set their calendars by the new moon, modern

Jewish holidays follow a specific Jewish calendar that differs from the popular civic calendar.

Rosh Hashanah

Rosh Hashanah is the Jewish New Year. This starts a ten-day period of reflection, meditation, sharing, and repentance. This holiday may include sounding the shofar (an instrument made from the horn of a kosher animal), eating challah (a braided bread), and partaking of apples and honey to represent a sweet new year. Apples, honey, and bread are also longtime harvest symbols honored by Pagans old and new.

Yom Kippur

Yom Kippur, the highest holy day of the year for the Jewish faith, happens a week after Rosh Hashanah. On this day, the Jews seek out those whom they have sinned against and make amends. The individual must determine the best way to do so him- or herself. This is also a time for forgiveness of others. For Pagans who meditate on the season turning from light to dark, this practice has strong spiritual parallels. While many Pagans do not define sin under the same categories as monotheists, most place strong values on personal responsibility including a sense of duty for making repairs when they have done harm.

The Feast of the Tabernacle (Sukkot)

Sukkot has the most direct connection of the September Jewish holidays with Mabon as it expressly celebrates the fall harvest. Always celebrated five days after Yom Kippur, this holiday observes the forty years that Jewish tribes wandered in the desert. Its literal meaning/command is "rejoice." Another name for this feast is Sukkot is *Chag HaAsif*, meaning "Feast of the Ingathering."

Simchat Torah and Sh'mini Atzerat

Immediately after Sukkot, the Jews celebrate the completion of the annual Torah reading. The Torah scrolls are taken from the ark that stores them, and people dance around them or carry them in a procession seven times. This concludes with a Torah reading—and thus completes the celebrations that mark the cyclical nature of the Jewish faith.

Thanksgiving

Thanksgiving is a descendant of Harvest Home festivals. It appears likely that the Pilgrims recreated the Harvest Festival feast that became US Thanksgiving. While not a universal holiday, Canada, Liberia, and Grenada also celebrate some form of Thanksgiving. Canada's Thanksgiving in October is a long weekend akin to the US Labor Day. Liberia observes Thanksgiving on the first Thursday of November; it is a mixed-religious holiday celebrated with foods native to the country. Grenada observes a Thanksgiving expressly to thank US military service people who intervened during a bloody military coup in 1983. Only the US and Liberian Thanksgivings have a direct connection to the results of the harvest.

Suggested Activities

Mabon is both celebratory and solemn. It also happens at one of the busiest times of year for many people. With themes of gratitude, death, grief, and looming winter, this is a time to acknowledge mixed feelings and do our best to tend to our inner balance. It's important to take time out to hear ourselves and hear the Divine at these action-packed phases of life. Because it is the harvest, it is also a spiritual act to go about routine organizing to make life flow all the more easily in the cold season.

Prepare for Winter

Even the most trivial action can become spiritual if performed with intent. Therefore, Mabon can be a day of spiritually getting organized. You may wish to partake in practical winter preparation activities: plant bulbs to bloom in spring, winterize your house, or even go over your calendars and to-do lists to ensure you can get as much as you can done in small chunks.

While outside planting or harvesting your garden, you may want to say a prayer or sing, just as the reapers used to when out in the fields. Celebrate your harvest and sing to the land.

A suggested prayer for winter bulb planting is:

SEED PRAYER
I sow the seeds
into the earth.
I send love;
I send yearning.
It fills,
it swells,
it reaches upward
toward the warmth
until the time comes
to burst from the soil
then to dance the dance of life.

Along with preparing your home in a practical manner, you may wish to sweep clutter out of your house to make room for the fruits of the new harvest.

Negotiate

September was a time of negotiating contracts and agreements for the harvesters of yore. Take a cue from them. Got something you need to work out with a credit card company, landlord, or service person? Use this time to hammer out a friendly agreement. Read up on negotiation tactics, and ask for a raise. Log in to your accounts and review your bills to see where you might get some breaks on routine bills such as utilities or insurance.

Can, Freeze, Pickle, and Dry

Harvest season often coincides with hunting season in temperate areas. For those with hunting families and big gardens, likely this regular activity goes back generations. Take a weekend to preserve the goods of your garden for winter. If you want to dry your own food, check a local thrift shop for a dehydrator. You can often find instructions for canning and pickling in cookbooks. Freezing preparation depends on what you freeze; different fruits and vegetables require different treatments. The Internet has plenty of information for all forms of food preservation.

Go Outside

If you live in a temperate climate, you likely already know how precious autumn is. Every day comes just a little closer to winter! Consequently, it's a good idea to get as much outdoor time in as possible! If able, go outside and walk in the woods. Enjoy the autumn foliage and observe how the animals act in preparation for this time. Perhaps take a nature guidebook and practice identifying plants at this point in the season. If you live in an urban area, check with your parks department. Most cities have some wooded land set aside for public use. If there isn't one, check a state parks guide for the nearest state park and enjoy a picnic among the trees.

Watch the Sunset

The sun feels especially precious in fall as the land becomes darker each day. Check your local newspaper or a good weather source to get the time of sunset and spend a week just sitting outside, watching it go down. You may wish to sing to it or perform a chant while you do.

Sunset Chant
Waning sun I feel you cooling;
waning day I see you darkening;
cooling, darkening winter comes
as the sun blazes away.

Watch the Sunrise

Sometimes finding time at sunset is just not a possibility. Early morning is the calmest time of day for most people. If you can, get up half an hour before the sun rises and watch its progress into the sky. You may want to do this every day until the next solstice, thus deepening your connection with the dark half of the earth's light cycle. Again, you may wish to sing to the sun or perform a chant while you watch it rise.

Sunrise Chant
Hail sun, light and arc,
fight again against the dark!

Honor the Harvest Moon

When the Harvest Moon happened in September depended on your location in Europe. Some thought of it as the New Crescent Moon in September, others thought of it as a full moon in August, and still others as the full moon in September. The Scottish nicknamed the Harvest Moon the Badger's Yellow Moon because it was the time that the small mammals collected winter supplies. They also sometimes called it the Hunter's Moon, as this was the time to hunt wild game for winter supplies. Create your own moon ritual according to one of these nicknames. You might also want to participate in a Scottish divination tradition, where young men and women assembled bundles of grain and stuffed them with peas and beans from their gardens, then burnt them. When the fire was down to glowing embers, someone hid a grain or seed amid the embers—the person to spot the seed was thought to have secured the love of his/her future spouse.

Host a Barbecue

Sharing food is a key activity of a harvest celebration. Invite other like-minded Pagans over for your own Mabon / Harvest Home dinner or invite your neighbors and simply enjoy the spirit of sharing. Serve food that suits the land where you live. In temperate areas, this may be wheat in the form of bread, corn on the cob, and fresh greens. If you're closer to the equator and you eat meat, serve animals that local farmers raise such as chicken, lamb, or goose. If you don't quite have the resources for a barbecue, invite people for a potluck. Make a list of recommended dishes for your guests to make, with the rule that each person should be able to eat what he or she concocts.

Roast Nuts

The eve of September 14, called Roodmas or *Fe'ill Roi'd*, was nicknamed "Night of the Nut." On this day, children went nutting—picking nuts for food. *Rood* referred to both the Christian cross and to deer rutting season (Campbell, 280).

Go Apple Picking

Start a fall tradition of visiting an apple orchard. While most go to the orchards to pick apples for their own canning and preserving, some offer other entertainments. For instance, some have apple canons that allow visitors to shoot an apple or a potato at a target, others offer hayrides, and some farms have also started producing local wines. Afterward, make a household ritual of preparing apple butter, making pies, or drying apples for the coming season.

Go to Wine or Beer Tastings

The festival of Dionysus has its own harvest mysteries, so if you are able to do so safely, partake! As more local vineyards proliferate in the United States, more are hosting autumn events inviting the public to come sample the season's vintage. As the craft beer movement grows, there are also more small breweries inviting people into their distilleries for tours. Wine and beer are sacred beverages in more than one Pagan pantheon, and Mabon is a great time to celebrate the artistry it takes to make them.

Build a Bonfire

Most harvest festivals concluded with a fire. Be sure to check with your city about legal restraints on fires in your area; this is one to skip if you live in an area of heavy droughts! If you get the all clear, gather up twigs, branches, and garden leftovers to build a fire. Have a great time roasting items on sticks in the fire, meditating on the flames, or dancing around it while singing or chanting. Perhaps distribute beverages to those with you and have a toasting game—toast to the health of the hosts of the fire, to everyone's prosperity, and then to everyone's good health. This is also a great time to tell stories. Stories about old-world faeries such as pookas or tales of King Arthur might be particularly appropriate.

Go Dancing

Many a harvest supper concluded with dancing. Nowadays, you can make this modern and have everyone go to a favorite club after dinner, or you can do something more traditional by trying to re-create Irish reels or perhaps watching a performance by a troupe of Morris dancers. For people familiar with the Burning Man, they might want to try "trance dancing" and put on music in a safe place and dance into and out of an altered state. The harvest was a time of expressing relief, and dancing can be quite cathartic!

Make a Corn Dolly

Celebrate with an effigy of the vegetative spirit, just as your spiritual ancestors did. Fashion a corn dolly out of wheat or create your own character out of fruits and vegetables you have grown yourself. You can find clear instructions with pictures and videos online. You can use the corn dolly as a centerpiece on your table during Mabon dinner; perhaps even keep it in a place of honor for the next year and ritually feed it by leaving small offerings in a bowl that you dispose of the next day.

You might also want to include the corn dolly in games that reflect the ones some reapers played during the harvest. In days gone by, people would hide alongside the pathway with buckets of water, waiting to douse the person carrying the effigy. As a modern twist, if having a ritual procession with the dolly, you might have your family or coven hide along its path with water guns, shooting at the doll and the person carrying it to represent the water needed for the next harvest. You might also weigh it down with stones, the symbolism being that the next year the harvest will be just as heavy as the stones.

Make a Wreath

Reapers often followed corn dolly processions holding wreaths on sticks. Make your own wreath using wheat or hay and decorate it with ribbons in the colors of the season. Hang it over your front door or on a door inside your house.

Visit Horses

In the Scottish Highlands, Michaelmas was also called Riding Day. There was always a horse race in Great Britain on this day with a man and a woman on each horse. Riders thought a woman falling off the horse was lucky. The women paid for the horse race and often brought large containers of oatmeal to share. Horse races are not as common in fall, but you might want to visit a petting zoo, farm, or rescue shelter and do something nice for a horse. You can top off the day by having oatmeal for dinner.

Have a Procession

Many localities had a procession at the beginning of harvest to cut the first sheaf and at the end of harvest after felling the last sheaf. Think of it as a parade without floats or fire trucks. It is a reverent if not necessarily serious affair. Because it has a playful element to it, it's an excellent ritual for children. The easiest procession you can do at home is to organize a parade to the garden, where you and your family perform harvest-gathering tasks. However, if you live in a city and do not have any garden space you can also adapt and draw from the Harvest Festival tradition of feeding the hungry.

The Garden Parade

This is a fun activity to have with children. Fashion an effigy from wheat or make a more standard scarecrow. Then draw straws or names to determine who carries the scarecrow to the field. Let the other family members get in line behind the person with the scarecrow. Have the person in the back pull a wagon (perhaps a child's red wagon) or carry a basket if your garden is small. Give your parade staff pan drums, rattles, and kazoos. If this might drive someone crazy, singing a song all the children know may be a better choice.

Lead the way from the front of the house to where the garden is while singing the song. If it's a short walk, take the procession around the garden a few times before signaling the leader to plant the effigy in the center of the patch.

When staked in the ground, say, "Praise to the land god!" and then everyone should cheer or make noise. Then say, "Praise to the harvest!" and everyone again makes celebratory noises.

From there, fill the wagon or basket with the products of your garden. Use the rest of the day to can, freeze, or otherwise preserve your garden goodies. This is a good opportunity to teach children old enough to be around hot stoves about these preservation arts. Set aside a few products of your garden for a shared evening meal with your family, and be sure to bring a few of your canned items to a community hunger organization.

Make a Harvest Basket

This is not quite the same as a procession, though you can encourage children to pretend it is. Take children to the grocery store and have them pick out nonperishable items for a local food shelf. Along with items such as canned fruits, vegetables, and meats, be sure to add items such as diapers and hygiene products. Assemble all of these in a basket. Conduct a short prayer around the basket, praying that those who partake of its contents receive good luck and bountiful harvests of their own in coming years. One such harvest basket prayer is:

Harvest Basket Prayer

Hail to the spirit of the land and to the spirit of the
    community.
Hail to the Goddess who gives all things!
We ask that you bless this basket of food and goods
meant to help those around us in need.
Let each item carry a blessing of good luck,
good health, good healing, and bountiful harvests.
Let our community be well and strong
by your hand and by ours.
So mote it be!

Participate in Pagan Pride

If Pagan Pride happens in your town, volunteer! Each municipality handles the event a little differently. Look online for your local coordinator and offer specific skills you can bring. If you work with a coven, grove, or other group, ask your fellows about performing a public ritual at Pagan Pride. If you are solo but want to connect, offer to run a ritual yourself! If the event doesn't happen where you live, consider starting one—the international Pagan Pride Project website is available to the public and its organizers can give you advice on starting your own.

Mabon Celebrations

No two sabbat celebrations look exactly alike. Even the exact time to celebrate Mabon differs across Pagan traditions. Some groups observe the sabbat on the full moon closest to the Autumn Equinox, or the UK Harvest Festival. Others try to place any ritual or feast as close to the actual moment of equinox as possible. Other groups use a "three days before or three days after" approach to accommodate coven members with busy work and family schedules.

These observances ideally include a shared meal and an acknowledgment of gratitude for sacrifices made. You can express this spirit in myriad ways: rituals are creative challenges. This is what makes Pagan faith practice enjoyable for many. With the themes of the harvest season and the sacrifice of a Divine king in mind, a coven or a solo practitioner can apply a great deal of imagination as to how these themes are expressed both inside ritual and in the greater world.

For instance, a feast may include food grown in the participants' gardens or food selected from any grocery store. What matters is that the food is seasonal to the area. In temperate climates, that might include squash, green beans, onions, peppers, and ground cherries. In areas closer to the equator, an Autumn Equinox feast might have cassava and plantains. What matters is that it reflects and connects to the ground you walk on every day.

Perform a Sacrifice

If sacrifice is the focal theme of your celebration, draw from how people experience sacrifice in modern life. Set up an altar with pictures of war heroes and emergency workers. Ask guests for stories about loved ones who made sacrifices. Write letters of thanks for those who made sacrifices for you. That might include parents who worked extra hours to help you finish your education, someone who took time off work to care for you while you were sick, or someone who donated blood or organs to save someone's life.

You may also wish to make a sacrifice of your own. Your action should fit the context of your life. There are causes that call for a person's time, especially causes that strengthen the whole community beyond your religious group. Perhaps you can offer a meal to friends unable to cook for themselves. You can volunteer at a local nursing home or with a road-cleaning crew. You might even take some of your garden abundance to your neighbors as a means of connecting your community to the earth you share. Hosting a barbecue corresponds to the Harvest Home sacrificial animal and is a familiar modern ritual. So is spending time at a dying person's bedside or giving up a few hours at the computer every night to help build a Habitat for Humanity house.

Make It Personal

You might start by picking one of Mabon's spiritual themes or integrating all of them to get the most out of this time of year. For instance, if you had a loved one die in the past year, you may want to create rituals and observances around mourning the passage of time and the dying light. You may feel especially grateful for what came to you by Harvest Tide; in that case, choose activities that express your gratitude and share your abundance. Acts of preparation for your own family or your community for winter (even if winter is hard times in hot weather) are excellent activities for this season. Most Mabon rituals involve expressions of gratitude, offerings made to the God and Goddess of the land, and a shared meal. You may wish to set aside a little bit of your garden or a little wine and beer for offerings and libations. If you feel especially flush, you might even gift someone from the labors of your own garden! Whatever you choose to do, celebrate Mabon to its fullest.

SPELLS
AND
DIVINATION

in resin - purification, prosperity, the mysteries of autumn a

ancestors, echinacea - healing, strengthening hyssop - purifie

...tion, patience, loyalty, eternal life, concentration, love myrrh

- purification, protection, spirituality, Solomon's seal - exor

...ing, purification, connecting to ancestors, connecting to land y

...ak - protection, luck, health, money, fertility. Pine - healin

- protection, prosperity, health, the sea Maple - love, frien

...m, prosperity, healing, prosperity, sleep Flowers carnation

marigold - protection, healing sunflower - purity, optimism

...re no stones specifically associated with Mabon. However, s

...s or sun deals are appropriate to this holiday. Animals, tote

...ding animals in the Mabinogion that helped lead & Arthur's

...rit world the Blackbird - one of the guiding animals in the

...sperity, men to Mabon; brings messages of other worlds to t

...of the guiding animals in the Mabinogion that helped lead

...hunting and wisdom the Eagle - one of the guiding animals

...land & Arthur's men to Mabon; associated with wisdom, insi

...almon - one of the guiding animals in the Mabinogion that

...alen of knowledge and past and future the Goose - asso

$\mathcal{M}$ABON IS A time of sweeping balance. As the light departs, it takes heat and memories with it. It is also a time to weave a new balance for yourself. If the past harvest went badly, this is the time to lay the groundwork for a better future. Use this time to rid yourself of obstacles inner and outer, and, like planting bulbs at the end of fall, start the deepest seeds for the most beautiful flowering when the world turns warm again.

Mabon Spells

The spells that follow are about putting your world in order. Just as our spiritual ancestors used the equinox to take account of their harvest and prepare for the winter, we call on that energy with these spells intended to correct the balance of the immediate universe.

A Spell to Find a Lost Object

Lost objects can happen at any time of year, you say? True. This particular season just happens to belong to gods who have successfully located children hidden from them. Helping you find your sunglasses, in comparison, should be easy. Invoking the spirits of wisdom that guided Mabon's men to him may not be necessary but are included as a last-ditch effort for those moments you just can't figure out where you put your car keys.

This spell actually fares better without a circle. You will need a pendulum—that can be any object you hang off a chain or a string.

First, tune the pendulum by holding it out and determining what direction means yes and what means no. To do this, hold it out in front of you and state how you desire that communication. Say, "Left for yes, right for no," or "clockwise yes, counterclockwise no," and so on.

Once you have established the yes/no system, stand in the room where you most likely lost your object. Hold your pendulum in front of you and ask, "Is the lost object in this room?" If the pendulum indicates no, try a different room until you get a yes answer.

If the pendulum indicates yes, pick a corner of the room and say, "Is my lost object close to this corner?" If no, try a different corner until you get a yes.

Once you get a yes in a quadrant of the room, hold the pendulum over each object in that area and ask for a report to see if it gives a yes or no answer. You may need to look under objects, move couch pillows, or shift furniture, depending on the strength of the pendulum's swing.

If you go through your house and only get a no, ask if the item is still in your house. If the answer is no, repeat this process in your car.

If you have not turned up anything, you may need to resort to a vision process. In this case, you will use a visualization. Settle yourself in a comfortable spot, preferably in the middle of a patch of sunlight. Visualize yourself surrounded by blue or golden light.

Then, in your mind's eye, see a blackbird. If the bird leads you to the stag, it is lost outside. Ask the stag the same question. See where the stag leads you. If the stag leads you to the owl, then someone has picked up what you've lost. Ask the owl. If it leads you to the eagle then the item has traveled from its intended location. Ask the eagle. If the eagle leads you to the salmon, the thing you lost may no longer be in its original form. The salmon will show you what form your lost object now takes. Whether you can replace it from there is up to you. Fortunately, most people won't need to go as far as asking the salmon.

A Spell to Promote Community Harmony

The conditions of our neighborhoods are living examples of whether a community has sown its seeds well or if it was faulty in its seasons of care. If we're born into the right situation, we can often find a good neighborhood to live in easily enough. For most of us, though, we either find a place we love only to find the people in it are less than interested in peace, or we must settle for what we can afford and hope for the best. So as autumn comes, harness that equinox energy to send the troublemakers to a place where they won't be so much bother.

Where we live affects how we think and how we view the world. It's easier to believe good things can come to you in a place where you can see good things coming to your neighbors. There's a lot of complicated history behind present conditions of a neighborhood and culture. If you are a part of that neighborhood and culture, then you are already a key organism within it. This gives you a right and a responsibility to influence the future of where you live for the greater good. If you live in a troubled neighborhood, equinox energy is a golden opportunity to sweep out the bad while bringing in the good.

This community harmony spell is one where you, in a very gentle way, influence the atmosphere. To do this, you need to create something to put into the atmosphere—a potion. When the liquid evaporates, it will carry with it the magickal charge you put in and in small, subtle ways bring about the more harmonious community you seek.

To make any potion you will need resealable jars or bottles, a funnel, coffee filters or cheesecloth, a pan, a wooden spoon, tap water, and the herbs desired.

Note: While purchasing from herb shops is ideal for most magickal practice, it is far from your only option. Keep an eye on the spice section at local grocery and dollar stores. You can also find great material in the ethnic food and tea/coffee aisles. If you had a great year in your herb garden, use that!

All potion making is simple: distribute herbs evenly on the bottom of the pan, pour in two cups of water, and stir constantly until the mixture is at a rolling boil. As you stir, perform a small chant while visualizing the mixture glowing a healthy pink. Once boiling, turn off the heat and allow the mixture to cool. Set the bottle or jar in your sink; line a funnel with a coffee filter or cheese cloth. Pour the potion a little bit at a time through the filter.

If your otherwise wonderful community had a bad year, you may want to help everyone along with a little magick. People with difficult lives often end up living near each other. Sometimes the damage sustained causes them to encourage strife instead of reaching to one another for healing and support. Sometimes the damage is so severe that it does not occur to them to reach within to do the healing work on themselves. Use this time to seed the chilling air with some healing energy so that it reaches your neighbors.

Use an herb mix of one part each (about a teaspoon) St. John's wort, juniper berry, angelica, cloves, and cedar chips.

Follow the directions above to create a potion. As you stir the mixture, chant:

> *Cleanse all poison;*
> *close all wounds.*
> *All who breathe this*
> *come, commune.*
> *Be well!*
> *Be well!*
> *Where we all dwell*
> *on this shared land*
> *all may excel!*

When finished, find a quiet time of night to pour the potion outside your home or near busy intersections and meeting places. You may wish to say something as you do this, linking it to the equinox: "Take the troubled with the dark, move them to where light can heal them."

A Spell for Community Prosperity

Sometimes a good neighborhood falls on hard times. In the days when almost everyone had a part in bringing in the harvest, it was obvious. Now the effects of bad harvests are more subtle but over time become visible. At these times when the known avenues dry up, it's important to kindle imaginations, to look into the unknown and see possibility rather than spending time gazing into the pool of things lost. Feeding such an atmosphere to the neighborhood spirit can bring surprises: hidden talents that the old work schedule suppressed, entrepreneurial adventures otherwise not taken, and a raw shared will to create anew. Despair and optimism can spread in equal parts, so when the darker side begins to spread you can respond by adding a hint of balance to the neighborhood's collective mood.

Use a mix of one part each of goldenseal and lovage root, and add three dried apricot ears. After you strain this herbal formula, you may eat the rehydrated apricot ears. Take in a little prosperity for yourself!

Then chant:

> *Goodness, come to us all!*
> *Good luck befall us all!*
> *New ways open, good things show*
> *within, without more treasures*
> *than we ever before did know.*

A Spell to Awaken the Activist Spirit

An engaged community is a great one, and a community that addresses the needs of the poor is an especially strong one. Since Harvest Festival nowadays feeds the hungry, and the Dionysian cult of old served those marginalized by society, Mabon carries a small activist charge within its energies. In urban centers, the seeds sown offer a harvest of creativity. When those centers become unhealthy, the absence of a healthy metaphorical crop leads to urban blight. Getting to the point where community members are using their passion for a collective good and finding the best place for their passion does take a bit of prayer, a bit of magick, and a bit of divine intervention. For some, especially those who have often met failure or obstacles in early efforts, it can take a rekindling of that passionate spirit that goes about making a change. Sometimes firing the spark within requires a simple, symbolic action, such as lighting a candle.

Candles, a staple in magick, are also a staple among activist communities. People hold candlelight vigils to remind us of those suffering elsewhere in the world. They pass lights to one another to represent the shared spark. What activists see as symbolism meant to imprint on the subconscious, others see as a direct act of magick. Both are right.

To cast this spell, gather a red candle, olive oil, salt, basil, cinnamon, and spearmint. First, mix a pinch of salt in a tablespoon of olive oil. Rub the solution on the candle from top to bottom, with the wick pointing away from you. This symbolically cleans the candle. Then, in another tablespoon of olive oil, mix a pinch each of basil, cinnamon, and spearmint. Rub this oil/herb mixture on the candle from the middle outward and then from the middle toward yourself.

Stand at your front door if it leads to the outside. If it is an interior apartment, either step outside on a balcony or go to a door that opens to the outside world. Light the candle and say:

Great God/ess, you have awakened me.
I see the changes needed;
the work that must be done to make them.
Gently, gently awaken the true companions in this task—
that we may share and live
and make our good together.
So mote it be!

Blow the candle out, and then repeat this every night for nine nights. On the last night, bring the candle inside and allow the flame to burn for nine minutes. Proceed to burn the candle for nine minutes a day until it has melted completely.

A Spell for Bees

This next spell isn't just for humans; it's also for bees. In an alarming and accurate return to tradition, if a farmer found a hive of dead bees, it bade a poor crop the next season. The disappearance of bees in recent years has underscored the literal truth of this—for those without vicious allergies, planting honeybee gardens might heal the bees and a good bit of humanity. Bees and honey were also a big part of European harvest traditions. The Europeans needed honey to make the mead for celebrations in the spring.

A honey jar is a piece of American folk magick (hoodoo) used to sweeten up a situation. In this case, you can use it as a bit of proactive magick to sweeten up the coming year and even to confer a blessing to your physical and metaphorical crops ahead of time.

Gather together a glass jar with a flat metal lid, honey or maple syrup, a pen (any color), paper (any color), sugar, sweetening herbs such as rose petals, cinnamon, nutmeg, lavender, or basil, and red, green, yellow, brown, or orange votive candles.

Have each member of your household write down what they know is coming in the next year and what they hope to see happen—asking the God/ess that it be as good as or better than they ask. When completed, put the letters in the glass jar. If letters become especially long, you may need to establish one jar per person.

Cover the letters with honey and add your mix of herbs. Speak a prayer over the jar(s) and say:

May the year be sweet and gentle,
honeyed and bright!
Bring abundance to all the things that sustain life!
So mote it be!

Seal the jar(s) as tightly as possible. Set the jar(s) inside an aluminum pan with a high edge/lip. On top of the jar, burn a candle: red for energy, green for growth and fertility, yellow for prosperity, brown for a peaceful home, or orange for happy surprises.

When the candles have burned down completely, bury the jars on your property. If you do not own property, find a favorite nature spot and set them in the ground before it freezes.

Mojo for Wisdom Spell

Wisdom often addresses the necessity of balance; it is what we call on to make the right decisions, just as people did at Michaelmas when deciding what to keep and what to release. Influence yourself toward wisdom with this mojo bag.

For this spell, gather a small, black velvet drawstring bag, five acorns, five rose thorns (optional), an image of a person who represents wisdom to you, a small owl charm, a handful of sunflower seeds, a 3-inch square of aluminum foil, and sage essential oil diluted in olive oil or rue-steeped sunflower oil.

Place the rose thorns (if you have them), sunflower seeds, and acorns on the aluminum foil and say:

> *Herbs, I bless you and awaken the wisdom*
> *you have to share with me.*

Fold the aluminum foil into a packet and place it inside the drawstring bag, then say:

> *Guide me to the wisest choices.*

Place the owl charm and the symbol of personal wisdom in the bag and say:

> *Help me see what I might miss,*
> *to question until I truly understand.*

Anoint the outside of the bag with a touch of the sage or rue oil. Then, tuck this bag into a clothing pocket or keep it in a hidden pocket on your coat or in the back of a purse. Take it out once a week and reanoint with the oil.

An Apple to Bless the Teacher Spell

Apples represent knowledge to Pagans in a different way than they do to Christians. If you slice an apple crosswise through the middle, you will see the five seed cores of the apple forming a pentacle—a symbol of wisdom and protection to many Pagans. Teachers, hopefully, are sources of wisdom and protection to their students and may need some protection in their jobs. So early in the year, pass an apple along to a teacher to enhance that sense of wisdom and safety that students and faculty both need.

In the early history of the United States, teachers were often barely older than the students they taught and relied on the parents of students for food and housing. Part of their pay consisted of food, so students would bring by apples and other foods from their parents' farms. The apple for the teacher became a symbol of the profession, although now teachers also ideally receive healthcare and retirement benefits instead of what food certain families can provide.

Teaching to this day remains a difficult job, whether in public or in private schools. Teachers all too often must dig into their own paychecks to provide school supplies while also using those same paychecks to fund the continuous education required to remain in the profession. In addition, they have few protections when students have violent outbursts, and they often catch any cold and flu that children bring in first. Those three months a year "off" are never actually vacation for most teachers—that's time used to develop lesson plans and work summer jobs. While not all teachers are dedicated, self-sacrificing people, the good teachers need our help. When they get that help, they strengthen not just our community but our shared future.

Since the beginning of most school years starts in fall (another extension of early American farm tradition) and the apple is already a symbol of Mabon and autumn, this small blessing falls into place. At the beginning of the year, assemble a basket of school supplies. You need not include actual apples, but decorate in an apple motif if you can. Include common classroom needs, such as reams of printer paper, glue, construction paper, scissors (all the better if you can get a few left-handed scissors in), facial tissue, hand sanitizer, baking soda, Lysol, crayons, pens, erasers, gel ice packs, dry erase markers, sticky notes, and perhaps a small bottle of one of those cold prevention remedies. If you are feeling especially generous, gift cards for phone and tablet apps can go a long way toward helping your child's teacher give the best education possible to his/her class.

As you assemble the basket, imagine the items glowing or taking on the personality inanimate objects do in an animated movie. Imagine each item spreading good humor, good cheer, and a sense of equanimity and passing that wisdom along to the teacher who runs the classroom.

Package the items up as well as you can and send a note along, thanking the teacher for his or her service to your children and to your community.

A Protection Spell for Community Protectors

In the United States, most townships rely on a network of volunteers and low-paid personnel to see to the safety of the entire community. What began as militia forces around the time of the Revolutionary War eventually became volunteer firefighters, first responders, paramedics, and involved community members who risk their lives in dangerous situations for the safety of others. The men and women who do this are the equivalents of the men and women reaping the harvest; their livelihoods meant security for the entire village. Seeing to their protection is a means of protecting ourselves; our world would be that much more difficult without them in it. These are the people who archangel Michael especially watches over, so performing this spell on September 29 (Michaelmas) is appropriate.

Some Pagans hold archangels in the same esteem that Christians do. Consequently, archangel Michael speaks to people of either faith. In the context of community and protection, Michael watches over warriors of all kinds, including soldiers, police officers, and peace advocates.

For this spell, you will need a pinch of dirt from the nearest police station, fire station, or hospital; a red candle; basil-infused olive oil; printed pictures of your city seal, the local police seal, the fire department seal, and the hospital logo; a printed image of archangel Michael; a heat-proof bowl; and spring water.

Place the image of archangel Michael on a flat surface. Then set the police, fire department, city, and hospital images in the bowl. Dress the red candle from the middle out to both ends with the herb-infused olive oil while asking archangel Michael to confer his blessing on your work.

Set the candle on top of the images and light it while speaking either the traditional prayer of Saint Michael or a version you are comfortable with.

A Pagan-friendly version might be:

> *Archangel Michael,*
> *you who watch over our warriors,*
> *keep them from evil, lead them to good,*
> *watch over them in their daily battles*
> *for the good of all.*
> *So mote it be.*

Dust the pinch of dirt over the images, and then pour the spring water into the bowl so that the paper is just covered. Add a little fresh water and repeat the prayer every day, relighting the candle daily until the candle burns out upon reaching the water level. Once done, bury the remainder of the spell either on your property, at the edge of a public park, or near a highway easement.

Corn Dolly Magick

Corn dollies were more than just symbolic to the harvest gatherers; to the reapers they represented real magickal energy.

In Europe, giving the dolly a place of honor for a year and then burying it or burning it at the beginning of a new harvest represented an important cycle—that dolly held the key to the condition of the next harvest. Even now, effigy magick is a powerful magickal tool; it need not represent a specific person or deity, but it can harbor the spirit of almost any intention you might have. Even if you do not farm, a corn dolly can bring about a harvest for you, whether you wish to sow a peaceful home, a safe neighborhood, or plenty of employment opportunity in the coming year.

Different dollies might have items added to them with sympathetic magick in mind. If you wish to make a corn dolly, you might also try some of the following decorations for it with magickal intent.

If you wish to see a new lover or marriage in the coming year, make two corn dollies—dress one like a bride and one like a groom (or two brides and two grooms, as appropriate.) Leave each one offerings of wedding cakes (you can buy sample pieces at most bakeries) or perhaps leave small offerings of mini-champagne bottles. Sing the bridal march to them and tuck pamphlets for honeymoon locations around them. If the new partner does not emerge in that year, burn them at the next autumn and start over again with new dolls.

If you wish to see greater fertility, abundance, or creativity in your home, pour water over the dolly once a day. In some parts of England, the last reaper carried the corn dolly home. Along the way, other villagers threw water on the reaper and on the dolly or sometimes dunked the dolly and the reaper together in a nearby stream.

If you want more money in the house, weigh down the center of the dolly with stones and weave ribbons into its body to represent hard work. If you practice a profession with a specific uniform, dress the dolly in a miniature version of that uniform. You might want to give it an apron, pens, computer or typewriter keys, or any other small symbol that imitates the work you do. Ritually feed it over the year by leaving it small offerings of honey, bread, beer, and apples. At the end of the year, dispose of it with burial or burning.

The most ancient of magick practitioners used what they had on hand. It's a good place to work from when designing spells. If you live in an area with lots of oak trees, for instance, use acorns, late season herbs, and colored leaves. If you live in an area with palm trees, you might want to use sand, palm tree leaves, or the broken stem of a succulent. If you stumble at crafting, you can also simply buy a package of cornhusks at a grocery store and stuff them with the other magickal symbols that serve your purpose. Pay attention to the subtle changes as the equinox passes through your part of Earth—then create your own spells using the things you witness change before your eyes.

Divinations and Lucky Charms

Our agricultural ancestors worried about the future just as much as we do. While we use tarot cards, meteorologists, and runes to find out what awaits us in the next season, those who went before relied on the tools around them to divine the future and perhaps to influence it.

Wine, Beer, and Water: Drink to Your Future

This comes from a playful Polish tradition, one of many in which someone tries to predict something about a future spouse. Better yet, it calls upon the three liquids of the harvest: wine, beer, and water.

This charm one partakes with a partner, preferably not a romantic one!

Set a glass of wine, a pilsner of beer, and a cup of water on a table. Then, sit with your back to the room so your expression can't influence your partner's choice—you may want to watch through a mirror. Have your partner come in after you and drink from any of the three beverages. If your partner drinks wine, you will marry rich. If beer, you will always have work. If water, you will stay single.

The Mabon Tarot Spread

You've heard the adage "as you sow, now shall you reap." This is a way to look at what energy you have put down and where it will lead—and what you will have to work with when your path has led in its own direction. All you need for this is a deck of tarot cards and space to spread them out. You may also want a camera to take pictures of your reading and a notebook to write out your gut responses.

This spread requires twenty-four cards total. You will spread and lay down cards in three groups of eight.

On the first shuffle, first lay down four cards. This represents what you have sown in the past. Then lay down an additional four cards directly beneath them. This is what you will reap because of the action referred to in the cards above it. Shuffle the cards and repeat the whole process two more times so you have three sets of cards to interpret.

The first eight cards represent your more distant past, things sown and reaped long ago. The second eight refer to your immediate past and present, and the last eight refer to your distant future.

There are very few fixed meanings in the cards. Usually only the Tower represents anything drastic, while Death represents permanent, deep psychological change. In this spread, however, a few more cards may appear, and because it is at an equinox, they may bear more weight than they do in the usual daily reading.

The Empress: This card is a signal of supreme fertility. If she shows up right-side up, all systems are go! If she appears inverted, however, you need to examine your relationships with the women around you. Ask yourself if you see mutual respect and shared power in the surrounding relationships.

The Chariot: This card can signal visitors or a journey. If it is right-side up, the querier may travel, and if inverted the querier may receive visitors. Since both can strain resources, look at the cards on either side of it to get any hint for a timeline.

Justice and Judgment: Justice is about having what is lost restored to you; Judgment is about the necessity of responsible actions. Often when one shows up in a reading the other follows shortly after. If Temperance appears near these cards, it is a signal that what has happened is a direct consequence of your own choices. If the Magician appears, you have the power to change it. If the Priestess appears, it is time to seek higher wisdom.

You can check photos and notes of your tarot reading from one harvest to the next. Make notes when you change course or seek additional wisdom—see how it affects your life over time.

Horseshoe Charm

An old superstition says finding a horseshoe is good luck. That makes sense as horseshoes are expensive! In old British tradition, a horseshoe affixed up above the barn door brought good luck (downward could pour out the luck—so keep those curves upward!) In modern day, affixing a horseshoe over a garage door or over a door that leads to the garage might also suffice. Perhaps this is not an overt harvest superstition, but it does remind us of our agricultural roots.

Michaelmas Daisy Divination

Remember playing "s/he loves me, s/he loves me not?" on some hapless flower? The game originally used the Michaelmas daisy, a small, white flower that blossomed in central Great Britain around the end of September. You can perform this divination on any flower. (Just make sure you don't take that flower from someone else's yard!) Ask any yes or no question, but don't cheat by counting the petals first!

RECIPES
AND
CRAFTS

...n resin - purification, prosperity, the mysteries of autumn eq...
...ancestors, echinacea - healing, strengthening hyssop - purifi...
...ction, patience, loyalty, eternal life, concentration, love myrrh...
...purification, protection, spirituality Solomon's seal - exor...
...ng, purification, connecting to ancestors, connecting to land y...
...k - protection, luck, health, money, fertility, Pine - healin...
...- protection, prosperity, health, the sea Maple - love, frien...
...m prosperity, healing, prosperity, sleep Flowers carnation...
...marigold - protection, healing sunflower - purity, optimism...
...e no stones specifically associated with Mabon. However, so...
...s or sun dials are appropriate to this holiday. Animals, tote...
...ading animals in the Mabinogion that helped lead Arthur's...
...rit world the Blackbird - one of the guiding animals in the...
...sperity, men to Mabon; brings messages of other worlds to th...
...of the guiding animals in the Mabinogion that helped lead...
...hunting and wisdom the Eagle - one of the guiding animals...
...lead Arthur's men to Mabon; associated with wisdom, ever...
...almon - one of the guiding animals in the Mabinogion that...
...dom of knowledge and past and future the Goose - associa...

$\mathscr{T}$HE ACT OF decorating, crafting, and cooking puts us in touch with rhythms happening on the planet right now. Our ancestors used what was available to express their creativity and joy. Mabon is about preserving beauty and appreciating abundance even as it fades from our grasp. We meet this challenge by using the things that fall on the ground to make art, and the things that go to seed to make food.

Recipes

Mabon feasts reflect Harvest Home feasts. They are as much a celebration of community survival as a family party. This is a good sabbat meal to invite guests to, especially guests that make your town safer, stronger, or smarter.

There is a school of thought that what should make the sabbats different from the esbats is food. While an esbat may have some ritual sharing of food—passing of symbolic bread, passing of symbolic wine reminiscent of Christian communion—the sabbat should host a full-on state of fellowship with food. For smaller groups, engaging the entire feast while still inside the magick circle is usually reasonably done, just expand the circle to include the table of food or use the serving table also as a focal altar. This, however, is impractical for those who participate in community celebrations. In most cases, for those who celebrate with groups of more than fifteen people, it is usually the best policy to conduct ritual and then to adjourn to the feast. Just remember your manners—always invite any deities you invoke to also attend the feast, and set aside a plate of food and a bowl for libations to ensure that if the gods wish to take their due, they may have it. If an interloper—human or animal—happens to eat the food, no worries. That just means that the gods wanted a taste.

Sometimes, people can't eat things. The rise of celiac disease and the popularity of vegan/vegetarian diets have made more than one coven/community celebration very tricky indeed. The gods are not nearly as inflexible as humanity. If you really cannot eat wheat or corn safely, they will understand. If you, for personal reasons, choose to abstain from meat or all animal products, just ensure you contribute something that the whole group can enjoy.

A post-ritual feast should be festive: that means focusing on the positive, what you like about one another, and finding things to like about one another.

Since this is a feast of gratitude, it is appropriate to perform blessings on the food. A routine food blessing might be "From whence ye came ye shall return; I thank you for what you are giving me." On other occasions, the right prayer for these occasions is "Good food, good meat, good gods, let's eat!"

Some groups cast a circle around the feast to make it part of the sacred space. If you choose to do this, make sure you include the bathroom and kitchen.

Harvest Bread

Bread is the quintessential harvest food. Its civilizing influence trails beer. It is almost a cultural universal. Europeans have bread loaves, Mexicans and some Central and South American countries have tortillas, the southern United States has corn bread, India and Pakistan have naan—the varieties, shapes, and forms bread comes in is infinite, as is the artistry in creating it.

Ingredients:
¾ cup warm water
1 package active dry yeast
1 teaspoon salt
1½ tablespoons sugar
1 tablespoon vegetable shortening
½ cup milk
3 heaping cups all-purpose flour
1 stick softened butter

Preheat oven to 375°F.

In a large bowl, add the warm water. Slowly stir in the dry yeast. Continue to stir until the yeast dissolves. Add salt, sugar, shortening, and milk to the bowl. Stir well. Mix in the first 2 cups of flour. If needed, begin adding more flour, one tablespoon at a time, until the dough chases the spoon around the bowl.

You do not need to use up all the flour called for in this recipe, or you may need more flour than is called for. The amounts vary depending on many factors, including weather, which is why most bread recipes only give an approximate amount of flour needed.

Turn the dough out onto a floured board and knead it, adding small spoonfuls of flour as needed, until the dough is soft and smooth, not sticky to the touch.

Use the softened butter to butter a bowl and a bread pan. Put the dough in the buttered bowl, and turn the dough over to grease all sides evenly. Cover and let rise in a warm spot for 1 hour. Punch down dough. Turn out onto floured board and knead again.

Form dough into a loaf and set it in the buttered bread pan. Cover and let rise for about 30 minutes. Before baking, score the dough by cutting three slashes across the top with a sharp knife. Then, put it in oven and bake for about 45 minutes or until golden brown. Turn the bread out of the pan, and let it cool on a rack or a clean dishtowel.

Ingredients:

1 pound green beans

1 can cream of tomato soup or 1 cup unflavored, unsweetened yogurt (dairy or soy)

1 tablespoon horseradish

1 teaspoon Worcestershire sauce*

¼ teaspoon salt

1 clove minced garlic

¼ teaspoon paprika

1 cup ground almonds

Preheat oven to 350°F.

Wash and trim the stem ends from the green beans. Place in a greased 8 x 8 x 2-inch baking dish.

In a medium bowl, mix cream of tomato soup, horseradish, Worcestershire sauce, salt, minced garlic, and paprika. Pour over beans and bake, covered, about 1 hour. Remove from stove and stir in the almonds, adding a layer across the top.

*There are vegan versions of Worcestershire sauce on the market; you can also make your own at home using molasses and vinegar as the base ingredients.

Bean Chili

Something about chili just announces "fall." It is a classic warm-up dish, one of those comfort foods that signals falling leaves and a season of impending traditions. Chili purists insist chili should be vegetarian. Add meat to the bean stew and you have *chili con carne*.

This vegetarian recipe is all about the bean and the pepper.

Ingredients:

¼ cup olive oil

2 cups chopped onions

6 garlic cloves, chopped (you can also save time by purchasing a jar of pre-minced garlic)

2 tablespoons chili powder

2 teaspoons dried oregano

½ teaspoon cayenne pepper (optional, for those who really like it hot)

3 15- to 16-ounce cans black beans, drained, ½ cup liquid reserved

1 16-ounce can tomato sauce

Heat the oil in a heavy, large pot over medium-high heat. Add onions and garlic; sauté until onions soften, about 10 minutes. Mix in the chili powder, oregano, and cayenne; stir 2 minutes. Mix in beans, the reserved bean liquid, and tomato sauce. Bring the chili to a boil, stirring occasionally. Reduce heat to medium-low and simmer until flavors blend and chili thickens, stirring occasionally, about 15 minutes. Season to taste with salt and pepper.

Roasted Beets

In recent years, a secret buried deep in the dirt emerged: beets are supposed to taste *good*. All that pickling and boiling kept the world from enjoying the wonder of them. Thanks to local food movements, however, this has changed. Roasted beets are on the menu and are they good.

Ingredients:
Two or more beets
Feta cheese
Walnuts

Preheat oven to 450°F.

Line a baking pan with aluminum foil. Rinse the beets. Remove the greens and set aside. (Beet leaves make an excellent salad ingredient.) Place the rinsed beets in the pan and roast until soft. You can test this by wrapping your hands in an oven mitt and slightly squeezing the beet—it will give just a little under the pressure. This can take between 45 and 90 minutes. After the beets soften, remove them from the oven and allow them to cool in the pan. Peel the beets—skins will come off under your fingers with a slight squeeze. Set the beets in a bowl and discard the skins and aluminum foil.

Slice and serve the beets. Garnish with feta cheese and walnuts.

Beetcake

Along with tasting sweet when roasted, beets make a fabulous butter and sugar substitute when baking. They do turn everything red unless you use golden beets. This recipe comes from experimenting with beets in desserts and main dishes. Red beets pair exceptionally well with dark chocolate.

Ingredients:
1 cup roasted, peeled beets
2 cups wheat or almond flour
½ cup cocoa powder
1 ounce unsweetened baking chocolate, melted
1 cup molasses
1 teaspoon allspice
1 teaspoon cinnamon
1 teaspoon ginger

Preheat oven to 375°F.

Place all ingredients in a food processor. Pulse until they form a cake batter consistency. Pour into a greased 13 x 9 baking pan. Bake until a toothpick or fork inserted comes back clean. Baking can take up to 55 minutes.

Apple Butter

Apples are the fruit of fall, especially in Europe and North America. Between the mythology of the fruit ranging from Eden to Troy and its seasonal benefits, it's almost a requirement at any Mabon feast. Like many an autumn crop, their abundance can take you by surprise—fortunately, many people have found clever ways to make the most of apples that goes far beyond dipping them in caramel or pressing them into cider.

Ingredients:
1 pound sweet apples peeled, cored, and sliced
2 teaspoons apple cider vinegar
½ cup maple syrup
¼ teaspoon ground cinnamon
1 / 8 teaspoon ground cloves
1 / 8 teaspoon ground allspice

Place the apples and vinegar into a large slow cooker. Place lid on top, set on high, and cook for 8 hours. Turn the slow cooker to low and continue cooking 10 hours more. After 18 hours, stir in maple syrup, cinnamon, cloves, and allspice. Cook another 4 hours. Scoop into mason jars and refrigerate until ready for use.

Baked Apples

Ingredients:
4 apples, cored
1 tablespoon raisins
1 tablespoon maple syrup
1 teaspoon cinnamon
1 clove per apple

Set apples on a microwave-safe plate. Inside the apple hollow, add maple syrup, raisins, and spices. Microwave the entire apple on high for up to three minutes. Serve immediately.

Apple Chips

Ingredients:
6 tablespoons confectioners' sugar
2 Granny Smith apples

Preheat oven to 225°F and line 2 large baking sheets with parchment paper.

Sift 3 tablespoons confectioners' sugar evenly onto the lined baking sheets. Cut apples into thin slices. Arrange apple slices in one layer on sheets and sprinkle evenly with remaining 3 tablespoons confectioners' sugar. Bake slices in the upper third of the oven, moving to the lower third halfway through baking, 2¼ hours total, or until slices are pale golden and starting to crisp. Immediately peel apple chips off parchment and cool on a rack. Apple chips keep in an airtight container at room temperature for 2 weeks.

Roasted Spiced Nuts

Nuts are so much part of traditional autumn that they have their own holiday. In England, September 14 actually became a day for children to go pick nuts! This nut gathering was called "going nutting." Almonds, pecans, and walnuts all emerge around Mabon, packing friendly protein and happy fat. You can get the most from nuts with the help of an oven or a food processor.

This recipe came about after an especially large bag of nuts languished too long in a cabinet. Nuts can keep indefinitely, even after cooking, but sometimes you just need the space. These make an intriguing alternative to croutons and crackers on soups and salads. The ½ cup of oil may seem high, but it's not—the excess oil is the best way to make sure the spices sink well into the pores of the nuts.

Ingredients:
½ cup olive oil (or sunflower oil)
1 teaspoon chili powder
1 teaspoon garlic powder
1 teaspoon paprika
1 teaspoon salt
1 pound nuts

Preheat oven to 350°F.

In a large bowl, mix the oil and spices. Stir in the nuts until coated thoroughly with the oil. Spread the nuts in an even layer across a baking pan. Cook for 8 to 10 minutes, or longer if you prefer a more caramelized result. After cooling on a paper towel, store in an airtight container. Enjoy as a snack or garnish.

Walnut Butter

This rich alternative to other nut butters is easy to make.

Ingredients:
1 cup walnuts
1 teaspoon walnut oil

Put at least one cup of walnuts in a food processor and pulse until the mix reaches a buttery/oily consistency. Help this process along by adding a teaspoon or so of walnut oil to the mix. Store the butter in an airtight container. Use on sandwiches or as a recipe substitute for peanut butter.

Ground Cherry Sauce

Ground cherries, or husk cherries, grow wild near roads in some parts of the United States and ripen in early autumn. They look similar to tomatillos with their husks. Once the husk comes off, however, the taste is completely different. They are sweet and unique, with a hint of citrus and strawberry. Many cooks are only now figuring out everything possible to do with them. Ground Cherry Sauce is one excellent option.

Ingredients:
1 cup water
1 cup white sugar
1 tablespoon vanilla extract
1 teaspoon cinnamon
¼ teaspoon ground nutmeg
¼ teaspoon ground cloves
4 cups ground cherries, husked

Place the water, sugar, vanilla extract, cinnamon, nutmeg, and cloves in a pan over medium-high heat. Bring to a boil, and stir in the cherries. Reduce heat, and simmer until cherries are transparent. Let cool until able to pour into resealable freezer bags and freeze, or pour into hot jars, leaving ¼ inch headspace. Adjust caps. Process the sauce (inside the jars) for 15 minutes in a boiling-water bath. Serve over sponge cake, ice cream, shortbread, or yogurt.

Pomegranate Mint Relish

Persephone famously ate six seeds from this fruit and was just in Hades about it. You will not have to suffer as she did.

The edible part of the pomegranate is its seeds. To get to them, slice off the top of the pomegranate. Then, slice the sides where you see the white chamber dividers. Pry open the pomegranate and remove the chamber dividers. Then you can simply pluck the seeds and eat them, pulp and all. You may wish to use a spoon to do this—the juice drips everywhere!

There are plenty of ways to enjoy a pomegranate either with an extract such as a juice or syrup or using the whole seed.

Ingredients:
½ small green onion, chopped
1½ cups pomegranate seeds (from about three fruits)
½ cup olive oil
1 tablespoon fresh lemon juice
1 tablespoon apple cider vinegar
1 cup finely chopped fresh mint
Salt and freshly ground pepper

Combine green onion, pomegranate seeds, olive oil, lemon juice, vinegar, and chopped mint in a small bowl; season with salt and pepper. Chill for at least one hour; can be made one day ahead.

Oranges with Pomegranate Molasses and Honey

You can buy pomegranate molasses at any specialty cooking store. If vegan, you can substitute the honey with maple syrup.

Ingredients:

8 large navel oranges. Peel and cut away white pith, then slice the oranges into thin rounds

¼ cup honey

3 tablespoons pomegranate molasses

½ teaspoon ground cinnamon

¼ teaspoon salt

8 large dates, pitted and chopped

Arrange orange slices, overlapping slightly, on a large rimmed platter. Whisk honey, pomegranate molasses, ground cinnamon, and salt in small bowl. Drizzle evenly over oranges. Sprinkle chopped dates evenly on the oranges. Let stand at room temperature.

Fig and Pomegranate Tapenade

Ingredients:
1½ tablespoons olive oil
8 ripe fresh figs, stemmed and halved
½ cup Kalamata olives, pitted and coarsely chopped
2½ teaspoons pomegranate molasses
2 teaspoons chopped fresh rosemary
½ teaspoon white vinegar
½ cup walnuts, toasted and coarsely chopped

Preheat the broiler. Line a small baking sheet with aluminum foil. Brush foil with olive oil. Lightly brush figs with ½ tablespoon olive oil. Arrange figs, cut side up, on sheet. Broil until figs are lightly browned at the edges, about 3 minutes. Cool on baking sheet.

Combine figs, olives, pomegranate molasses, rosemary, and vinegar in a food processor. Using on/off turns, coarsely chop figs and olives. With motor running, add the remaining tablespoon of oil. Season to taste with salt and pepper. Transfer to bowl. Stir in walnuts. Let tapenade stand 2 hours at room temperature to blend flavors. (Can be prepared 5 days ahead. Cover and refrigerate. Bring to room temperature before serving.)

Serve with bread, crackers, or on apple slices.

Mabon Crafts

Pagans are often crafty people, as easily enticed by the promises shining in a bead store as they might be in any occult bookshop. As a result, often enough, art is magick and magick is art. Much of this universal weaving begins while crafting. The autumn season especially speaks to a magickal crafter's heart, so many supplies literally grow on trees and fall to the ground at this time!

Crop Art

Crop art uses parts of a plant to create an image in place of paint. You can use seeds, beans, and other pieces of dried plants to create mosaic images and sculptures. This can give you a whole new set of things to do with any leftover seeds from your garden! You may wish to use things you grew yourself to make such a mosaic to commemorate each harvest; those who live in apartments might also enjoy obtaining seeds and dried pieces from local farmers and creating a mosaic as a link between their own homes and that of the greater community.

What you'll need:

- Seeds, whether all the same or different shapes and sizes. If you use a single seed type, plan to focus on the shape of an object rather than adding details. Rice, beans, corn kernels, sunflower seeds, seeds released from garden plants, and pieces of dried straw are just a few examples of your choices.

- A flat, dry surface such as cardboard, poster board, canvas, or almost any other material. You may even want to cut open an old cereal box and use that cardboard as your seed canvas.
- A pencil or a piece of chalk
- A paintbrush
- A spoon
- Glue, such as Elmer's craft glue
- An adhesive fixing spray for when your project is complete
- A well-ventilated work area

On the chosen canvas, sketch out the image you want to create in either chalk or pencil. Use the paintbrush to paint glue inside the lines. Carefully press your seeds and other plant matter onto the glue. You may wish to define each section of the image with a different plant. For instance, if you want to depict a mermaid with red hair, use lentils for the hair and dried green peas for the tail.

Some artists like to add paint coloring to the seeds after the glue has dried.

If you want a permanent piece of art, add a spray adhesive after the glue has dried. If you prefer to return the art to nature after Mabon, and if you used a biodegradable canvas, you can cut the image apart and bury it either on your property or in flowerpots if you want to see what it might sprout.

Scarecrow Effigies

Of all the sabbats, Mabon calls the loudest for an effigy. Effigies are in the same magickal family as poppets but larger and often made of plant matter.

What you'll need:

- An outfit of old clothing—pants and a shirt
- An old pillowcase; grocery plastic bags may work as well
- Dried leaves for stuffing
- A 6- to 8-foot-tall pole
- A 5-foot-tall pole (to use as a cross stick)
- Clothespins or safety pins
- Twine
- A marker

First, stuff the plastic bag or pillowcase with leaves. This will form the scarecrow's head. Close off the bottom with clothespins, safety pins, or a bit of twine. Next, insert the head onto the longer pole by inserting the pole into the "neck" and stopping just as it hits the top of the head. Slide the shirt (at the neck) up the pole until it meets the head. Attach with safety pins or clothespins. Use the location of the shirt and the armholes to determine where to affix the 5-foot pole. Use the twine to attach the 5-foot pole as arms.

RECIPES AND CRAFTS

Then, pull one leg of the pants up the pole and position under the shirt. Attach at the hem and the waist with safety pins or clothespins. Tie off the other pants leg with twine and stuff with dried leaves. Take a piece of twine and run it from a belt loop to underneath the shirt. Bring the twine back around and tie off in the belt loop. Repeat on the other side. Push the pole into the soil so you can stuff the scarecrow upright. Stuff leaves into the shirt, through the armholes and into the pants. Tie off all openings. Using the marker, draw a face on the scarecrow. If you plan to use him as a ritual effigy, a solemn or even somewhat dismayed expression is appropriate. Attach hats, scarves, and other accessories desired with safety pins.

Mabon Oil

You can use this oil to anoint your sabbat candles or to bless the small effigies you make with the power of the day.

What you'll need:

- 1 tablespoon sunflower oil
- 1 pinch white sage leaves
- 1 pinch rosemary leaves
- A few apple seeds

Combine items in a glass jar or vial. Leave jar in the sun for two to three days.

Mabon Incense

This is a loose incense, meaning you only need to mix the herbs together and drop a pinch on a piece of incense charcoal or into a fire.

Ensure all herbs are dried. If unsure, spread the herbs out on a cookie tray and heat inside a stove set to 250°F for 90 minutes.

What you'll need:

- Pinch marigold
- Pinch spearmint
- Pinch sage
- 2 to 3 cloves (per personal preference)

Mix together one pinch marigold with equal parts spearmint and sage. Add 2 to 3 cloves to the mix. Make sure that all plants are totally dry before mixing.

Store the jar of incense in a cool, dry place until ready for use.

Mabon Bath

Ritual baths use herbs as a way of attuning the bather to the ritual ahead. If you do not own a tub, you can also pour mixtures over your head or brush a powder over your body.

What you'll need:

- 1 tablespoon sage
- 1 tablespoon rosemary
- 1 tablespoon chamomile
- Cheesecloth or small-mesh strainer
- ½ cup sea salt
- 1 tablespoon baking soda
- Sandalwood essential oil

In a saucepan, prepare a decoction of sage, rosemary, and chamomile over medium-low heat. Simmer for 3 minutes. Allow to cool, then strain the liquid into a plastic jar or bottle. (This is for safety—bathrooms are slippery, and glass in a tub is dangerous.)

In a separate jar, mix together sea salt and baking soda. Add a few drops of sandalwood scented oil. Store the bath salts in a shatterproof jar.

When ready to take a bath, fill the tub with water. Before entering, pour in the sea salt mixture and then the liquid preparation. Stir the bath water until the salt crystals dissolve. Once dissolved, bathe as usual.

Apple Candleholders

Apples ripen in the fall and sometimes a bag of apples has more than a family can eat. Rather than just let them rot, add a little function to your altar decoration with apple candleholders. When you finish you can eat any part of the apple without wax drip.

This works with taper, votive, or tea light candles—slightly better for the latter two.

What you'll need:

- A paring knife
- As many apples as desired
- A spoon

Cut about a half an inch off the bottom of the apple to ensure there is a flat surface.

Next, cut a circle around the top stem of the apple. Then, cut off the top of the apple around the circle lines, just below the stem center. Take a spoon and scoop out the apple center until you have removed enough flesh that the candle will fit.

At the end of ritual, compost the apples or eat them!

Acorn Prayer Beads

Lots of rituals and spells prescribe a chant and a number of times to repeat it. Sometimes it's difficult to keep track. While any bead or coin system may work, Mabon season presents nature's own beads—acorns! Gather as many acorns as you like and sort them into groups. For instance, often chants happen in sacred number groupings, such as three, seven, nine, or thirteen.

What you'll need:

- Acorns, as many as possible
- String
- A small drill (hand drills are good for this)
- Scissors

Set aside the specific number of acorns you want for your prayer string. Cut a piece of string for each acorn grouping. Drill a hole through each acorn. String each acorn and knot both ends.

You may want to fill the end acorns with a large drop of hot glue to prevent them all from sliding off the string.

Acorn Worry Dolls

What you'll need:

- Acorns
- A small drawstring bag

In Guatemala, children and adults suffering from insomnia fill a little bag with tiny, colorful dolls. The insomniac takes out each doll and tells it one worry. As this person sleeps, the doll carries away the worry. The Guatemalans are not the only people to use a little magick to address anxiety; ancient Greeks rubbed thumb-sized stones as a means of easing tensions.

Our ancestors used what they had around them for their magick, and we can do the same. You can simply gather acorns into a small drawstring bag—like a worry doll, tell each one a worry. If an acorn disappears, just assume it's gone off to take care of something for you.

Leaf Candleholders

This one is great for beginning crafters. A Mason jar candleholder offers wind protection, decoration, and when finished, candle storage!

What you'll need:

- A Mason jar
- Craft glue
- Dried and flattened autumn leaves
- Paint brush

You may want to press leaves between the pages of a book for a few days before using them for this project.

Paint the inside of the jar with the glue. Gently press the leaves to the glue, with the side you want showing toward the outside. White glue dries clear, so yes, you will see the actual leaf color on the other side of the glass. You may want to use a chopstick to smooth the leaf to the glass.

Allow the jar to dry for about two hours. Drop in a tea light or votive candle. Make sure you pay attention when burning candles in the jar: leaves can catch on fire and glass can get very hot!

Stick Figures

Remember that old "don't know how to draw" go-to, the stick figure? Lines represented body parts with a circle on top for a head. If you felt fancy, you added a hat.

Now you can make a stick figure out of real sticks! You will find plenty on the ground as you gather autumn leaves for other projects—and this offers you a comfortable alternative to the skill it takes to fashion a corn dolly.

You will need:

- 5 sticks, no more than 6 inches in length
- Leaves, acorns, or flower petals you might wish to add
- Glue (a glue gun or standard craft glue works fine)
- Newspaper

Gather twigs fallen to the ground, along with leaves, bark, and any other natural material you want to make your stick figure.

Set out newspaper on a flat surface. Lay one stick in front of you. Arrange the other four sticks a few inches apart at a slight diagonal to represent the arms and legs. Glue the sticks in place. Add a leaf at the top of the first stick. Glue in place. Add and glue flowers, acorns, and so on. You may wish to glue on googly eyes or use a marker to draw a face. You can use this as a poppet or even as a miniature effigy. Treat your stick figures with kindness.

Wreath of Real Leaves

Wreaths as adornment go as far back as the Ancient Etruscans. In Etruria, rulers wore them as crowns. The ancient Greeks wore them to indicate occupation and social rank. They also made a wreath, woven from harvest plants, then hung it on the door until the next year. The wreath also appeared as a crown or as an indicator of the finished harvest during Harvest Home celebrations—so it seems fitting to make one to hang on your own door! The real leaf wreath consists of preserved autumn leaves. It has a more lightweight feel than traditional variations; because of this, when you hang it you may want to add some extra-strong double-sided adhesive to make sure it stays.

What you'll need:

- About 50 autumn leaves
- A large pan—square baking pans work well
- A pan that fits inside the larger pan
- ¼ cup vegetable glycerin (this helps preserve the leaves)
- ½ cup water
- Glue or a needle, scissors, and thread
- A spoon

In the larger pan, mix the glycerin and water with a spoon. Add the leaves to the solution. The liquid should completely cover the leaves. Place the smaller pan on top of the leaves. Allow the leaves to sit in the solution for 3 days. On day 3, remove leaves from the solution. Pat dry with cloth or paper towel. You may wish to allow leaves to dry an extra day or two after. Glue or stitch the leaves together in a circular pattern.

Allow glue to dry before hanging the wreath. You can preserve the wreath between seasons by storing it in a box between sheets of wax paper.

Gratitude Journal

Mabon is a season about celebrating having what you need and is very much aligned with Thanksgiving holidays celebrated in some countries. This makes it an excellent time of year to start a gratitude journal. Once a day, write down in a special notebook something you feel grateful for. Some days you may have more than one. Other days you will struggle to think of one thing. Forge ahead with it. You may even want to decorate the pages, doodle on them, or include pictures, short stories, and anecdotes about the things you feel grateful for. It is okay to mention something you feel grateful for more than once.

All you really need for this is a notebook and a pen. You can add other material as suits you.

Mabon Decor

Decorating is a way to attune yourself to the passing of the seasons, whether you simply change the candle colors on your altar or bedeck the house in autumn colors. Stores abound with seasonal decor choices: if you can just buy what you need to bedeck your house, you can enjoy that. However, if you wish to make traditions visceral, creating your seasonal home decor is a way to make the sabbat and your own home that much more personal. Children especially love crafts; it's a good way to engage them with household faith traditions that allows them to understand the household rituals in a concrete way.

Mabon decorations should reflect mainstream autumn decorations. Colors are typically in reds, yellows, oranges, muted greens, and browns. Leaf and tree motifs are common, as is the appearance of wheat, corn, rye, and seeds. All the natural material that falls to the ground in autumn makes great Mabon decor. Some people like to use cornucopia themes at this time for the Mabon association and because the shape is thought to attract abundance.

Some people prefer to make their own decorations or even to craft functional items for their practice. Making magickal tools is time-honored though not a requirement. You may wish to explore the Internet for even more Mabon and autumn crafting ideas.

In the case of the harvest sabbats, food is an essential feature in ritual. Pagans are not just giving thanks for the nourishment of the earth but thanks for the gods revealing the mysteries of agriculture to humanity so that we might have a way to prepare for winter and for our survival of the harshest conditions the year can give us.

PRAYERS
AND
INVOCATIONS

n rose - purification, prosperity, the mysteries of autumn

ancestors, echinacia - healing, strengthening hyssop - purific

ction, patience, loyalty, eternal life, concentration, love myrrh

- purification, protection, spirituality, Solomon's seal - exo

ng, purification, connecting to ancestors, connecting to land

ck - protection, luck, health, money, fertility, Pine - healin

- protection, prosperity, health, the sea Maple - love, frien

ns, prosperity, healing, prosperity, sleep Flowers carnation

marigold - protection, healing sunflower - purity, optimism

re no stones specifically associated with Mabon. However, s

s or sun deals are appropriate to this holiday. Animals, to

ading animals in the Mabinogion that helped lead Arthur'

rit world the Blackbird - one of the guiding animals in th

sperity, men to Mabon; brings messages of other worlds to

of the guiding animals in the Mabinogion that helped lead

hunting and wisdom the Eagle - one of the guiding animals

lead Arthur's men to Mabon; associated with wisdom, use

lmon - one of the guiding animals in the Mabinogion that

lon of knowledge and past and future the Goose - asso

*P*AGANS DO NOT usually use catechisms or have central liturgies in their theologies. This means we do not have official invocations and prayers. What we have instead are homemade invocations based on epic poems, Homeric hymns, and the basic concept of asking nicely. All of what follows are simple invocations and prayers; you may insert them into rituals you are writing, write rituals around the invocations, or use them as a template to follow when constructing your own invocations.

When writing any invocation or prayer, it is important to pay attention to the details of a given god. For example, you may want to invoke Athena—but Athena has many aspects. Are you seeking the scholar, the feminist icon, the warrior, or the instructor in humility? All at once may be more than you can handle. Spend time reading and familiarizing yourself with a god before you invoke one or make requests. Some gods will not want to fill your requests and others will have no interest in the ritual or in you. It is often enough a matter of resonance. Listening to your gut—rather than just imaginings—can lead you to the right personality for the right job and give you an idea about the right way to give thanks/energy back for that assistance. However, especially for those new to ritual practices where the gods get to talk back to you, it can take some time to hear those gods and to develop that gut instinct. Research can take you where intuition is not ready to go.

Before starting an entire ritual invoking a deity, take some prayer and meditation time to introduce yourself to that being. Some of the invocations here may be used for this purpose. Cast a circle, speak the invocation, and then verbally ask for communication time to get to know one another. Accompany this with an offering, whether a libation or burning incense or a candle. Whether or not these offerings are more effective or better energy, they are usually good etiquette.

While pop culture often has playful takes on the personalities and traits of the gods, it's a good idea to go look at the sources that fed those modern creations. So, as wonderful as Hercules and Xena may be, still try to go to the source material first. Look to what the ancient Greeks wrote about their gods, what the folklore of the Mabinogion described when it came to Celtic gods, to the Bhagavad Gita for the Hindu pantheon, and so on. Bear in mind as you read and meditate on these deities that their cultural context is rooted in their culture of origin and some may see things in a way much different than what you know. Even if your concept of gods and godforms is strictly metaphorical, it is still a good idea to consider this if only to evaluate how such invocation may affect your own subconscious patterns.

If looking for better information before invoking a deity, consider using the Internet to find as much source material as possible:

Internet Sacred Text Archive: http://www.sacred-texts.com/

Google Books: If you use the "search tools" box, you can set your search to Free Google eBooks. This holds many books from the nineteenth to the twenty-first century, some of which contain public domain material with some of the earliest known information about different gods and cultures.

Ishtar and Tammuz: Ishtar and Tammuz bear special celebrity in Western culture: they are among the Pagan gods mentioned in the Old Testament of the Bible. In particular, one of Tammuz's seasonal rituals involves women in the fields crying over the soil as a symbolic act of mourning his death. Even so, we know the least about the rituals of Ishtar and Tammuz. If you choose to invoke them, go slow—they, more than any included in this book, require a ritual of introduction.

An Invocation to Ishtar

Queen of Heaven,
we look toward the eagle
to send our messages of love to you.
Great Mother, priestess of the skies,
be gentle with us;
pour your rain upon our fields
as once you wept for Tammuz.
Cradle us, that though we reach skyward
we do not hurtle to the earth
but come to it gently
when our fallow times come.

An Invocation to Tammuz

In our tearful moments, we plant our seeds
as you, Tammuz, lay beneath the earth to receive them.
It is in joy that we shall sow them,
the joy that rises
from going deep,
lying still beneath
then rising, reaching for the light.
We stretch, we grow,
your return betides
the end of every dark night,
every winter

of the soul.
Shepherd us, your people,
tend us well,
so that we may tend your body
fallen upon the land.

An Invocation to Demeter

Demeter is the great mother goddess and the keeper of the Eleusinian Mysteries. Mabon is a profound time for her, Persephone, and Pluto. While much grain goddess lore focuses on her effect on agriculture, her stories offer many lessons about empathy and compassion as well.

Mother of the grain, mother of all that grows,
we reach out to you, offer our arms,
return your comfort with our comfort,
your love with our love,
your loss with our loss.
We open ourselves to your Mysteries,
align,
listen,
observe.
We will rejoice with you as you rejoice.
Blessed are your Mysteries.
Blessed are your Mercies.

Blessed are you,
Mother of the Wheat,
Goddess of the Corn,
She who turns the seasons
by sun, by fire, by wind, by rain.
We await Persephone's return with you.
We honor your lessons as we work the earth.

An Invocation to Kore

Sweet maiden at the edge of the earth,
fear not.
You have the strength of all women within you.
You have the power of your loves to sustain you!
As you descend,
our hearts descend with you.
In all our human yearnings
it is you who we seek—
your thought that warms us in dark nights.
You help us remember
the mysteries of springtime,
the light that warms the soil,
the grace of wonder
as we behold the miracles of this world
even as missing you is bittersweet.
We look forward to rest in the dark.

It is as you are beneath
that we may rest.
We shall greet you at the edge of earth
as snow sinks into soil
to hear of your lessons for us;
to behold you, as woman.

An Invocation to Persephone

Queen of the underworld,
we greet you
with libations, fruit, honey, perfume.
Speak
so we may hear the voices of our ancestors
as the land goes dry and dark.
Yellow paths
mark your trails of descent.
We give you now
what we would lay to rest;
we render the pain, the love
stored in our breasts
unto you, O Queen of the Dead.
May our own hearts be light
when we meet you.

An Invocation to Pluto

King of Hades,
he who keeps what lies beneath,
we hail to you
who receives what we send to the earth.
Pray judge it well,
be merciful when we stand before you,
reaping at last
all we have sown.
We lay these old pains to rest before you.
Take them with you, king,
and send them to their rightful place.

An Invocation to Pluto and Persephone

Hail to the King and Queen,
ruler of the dead,
voice of the dead!
Receive our messages of love
as all around us
ages, lays still,
surrenders itself to your care.
We send to the earth
that which in rest may grow,
that which you might keep awhile in the Land of the Dead.
Be merciful, King and Queen—

take only that which must be taken
that we may live another season here.

An Invocation to Mabon

The Celtic Mabinogion refers to Mabon as the son stolen from "between his mother and the wall." Aidan Kelly believed that Mabon's disappearance paralleled Persephone's kidnapping and that Modron was a deified version of the land the Celts stood upon—making Mabon a literal son of the earth and part of cyclical mysteries.

Hail, Mabon, son of Modron,
exalted prisoner!
Reveal the hidden things,
guide us through the path
to that which is hidden,
to memories long forgotten.
Show us what lays beyond the castle wall.
Send the blackbird to sing to us,
send the stag for us to chase,
send the owl for us to listen,
send the eagle for us to see,
send the salmon to tell us
how to set free the hidden thing.

An Invocation to Modron

Great Mother, goddess of the land,
we see your grief and we honor it.
We see your love and we cherish it.
In our silences
let us hear the land,
so we can hear your voice
speaking
between the ocean and the winds.

An Invocation to Dionysus

Ancient Greeks revered Dionysus as the master of mysteries
of the vine, just as Demeter held sway over the mysteries of
grain. His worship in ancient Greece involved the ecstasy of
wine.

Hail to the king of the vine!
Semele's son, it is the ecstasy you provide
that relieves us from the grief of living.
In the grape comes the balm to sorrows,
so that when we return to the sobered world
memory of such merriment
makes our losses not so harsh;
our pain not so great.
You are he who uplifts the poor,

who elevates women,
who frees slaves
and those enslaved too.
Double-doored god,
born twice of woman and man,
we pour out our cups to you,
pound our feet to the soil for you!
In this wine, in this juice,
we partake of you.
We dance to your ecstasy
in sunlight.
We dance again
as the rain pours itself onto the earth
as you so poured yourself into the vine,
as you once poured your being into us—
we are full of you,
and so we fill you.

An Invocation to Bacchus

Some people consider Bacchus and Dionysus interchangeable. The Romans did do a good job of establishing a syncretic religion that only minimally disrupted the cultures brought into their empire. Even so, differences did occur. On an intuitive level, Bacchus can feel like a different personage from Dionysus, though one might recognize the other as a sort of shadow self.

If performing invocations and prayers, it only seems right that Bacchus have a prayer separate from that of Dionysus.

You can find translations of hymns to Bacchus online. Here in its place is a twenty-first-century variation on the original hymn:

Hail Bacchus, voice of thunder,
horned one of field and farm,
bull of heaven!
He who raises passion,
consumes with it,
teaches with it,
releases it.
Praise to you, immortal king,
grant our supplications
that we may have cause
for celebration, for singing of your praises,
as what we grow
can kindle passions
and rejoicing
for seasons to come.

An Invocation to Apollo

Pagans often see the sabbats as the solar holidays while esbats celebrate the lunar cycles. Mabon, as an equinox is especially solar, and so some Pagans choose to honor gods of the sun at that time. The ancients were keenly aware that the sun is crucial to the health of all crops. Without enough sun, plants do not get what they need to live. With too much sun, they wither and die. Consequently, Apollo received his own section of harvest celebrations.

Hail to Apollo!
We salute you
as you pull your chariot across the sky.
With a kiss from our palm to you,
we send our praise!
We feel you cooling to us
as it must be
from time to time
between lovers.
Come spring,
we too shall be eager for you—
to feel your touch on our skin,
to see what you alone
can raise from the soil.
Fare thee well into the autumn, Apollo.
We love the glimpses we get
of your shining countenance
behind the greying sky.

Invocations to the Goddess and God

Many Pagans accept the idea of individual gods and goddesses or the idea of one God/ess with many faces. Some still prefer to pray to or invoke what they see as the whole—God/ess or at least address the God and the Goddess (or Lord and Lady) as separate entities.

GODDESS

Blessed Goddess, Mother of all that is,
we ask that you bless our harvest,
and that you bless all that results
of seeds sown in this year.
Your abundance is infinite;
your presence eternal.
Please, by your grace,
give us the power to give back to you
as you have given to us.

GOD

Blessed Consort, we greet you
with tears and with praise.
It is your kindness
that allows us to live;
your sacrifice
that reminds us to care for others—

to extend that caring
outside our own tribes.
You have lain down for us,
led us,
lived for us.
We take your teachings,
take your nurturing,
and weave our lives together
for the good of all,
as you have done
for the good of us all.

LORD AND LADY
Lord and Lady,
even you, the most holy of all couples,
must let death steal away.
We see this, we know this.
Lord, we bid you well on your journey.
Lady, we bid you safe return.

Invocation to the Dark Night of the Soul

The Spanish mystic Saint John of the Cross penned the poem
"Dark Night of the Soul" around 1579 to describe the soul leaving the body and achieving union with God. The title of the
poem is now used by mystics of many religions (and by a few

therapists) to describe people experiencing extreme difficulty in life to such a degree that those who are religious—and some who are not—experience a loss of faith or spiritual crisis. While the original author saw this ultimate dark night as death, some Pagan faiths believe that people can experience death in a metaphorical manner as much as in a physical one.

Those in spiritual crisis may especially struggle with Mabon. The holiday revolves around the themes of gratitude and sacrifice with a heavy emphasis on bonds of love and community. For a person enduring such a crisis these themes may feel burdensome.

No single prayer can speak to the complexities of every situation. During crisis, prayer may not appeal. Honesty, at least, can perhaps relieve a little bit of the inner pressure—even in the form of an honest prayer. One suggested prayer is this (it may help to speak the prayer out loud):

God/ess,
I want to be grateful.
I wanted to be grateful.
I might even understand
how your sacrifice has brought us here.
As much as I want to,
I can't feel it right now.
I see the rejoicing,

but my heart does not stir—
I cannot even remember that time when it did.
Right now I am in pain.
It dulls the senses,
dims connection.
I can't even see you
through all my wounds.
I feel abandoned, ignored, hurt
by you and by what surrounds me.
I am unsure if what I seed
has any reward at all.
Will you return to me?
Were you ever here for me?
Is there something that needs your forgiveness?
I need your love, God/ess.
I need your compassion.
In this moment, I speak my truth:
I doubt. I distrust. I hurt.

Giving Thanks

Ultimately, Mabon is about gratitude. There are many times and ways to express gratitude and it is really a daily part of Pagan life. Mabon is the ultimate holiday for it, before we again move into other deep mysteries of life—sometimes even the feeling of thankfulness can be a mystery in itself.

Gratitude Prayer

God and Goddess, you who make the tides turn,
who shift the energies at the tilt of the earth,
we thank you for your kindness and abundance.
Let us remember you and remember each other
in the coming winter:
it is not just food and water that sustain us,
but the connection of heart to heart
that carries us through our winters.
We ask that you bless this meal
that we may carry the best possible blessings
and connection with one another
in the coming year.
Blessed be!

Gratitude Prayer for the Crop

Lord and Lady, with thanks and praise,
with libation and burning incense,
we celebrate the gifts that weigh on our table.
The gift of each other
that has come with us from one year to the next,
from one season to the next,
from one day to the next,
even from one moment to the next.

We are here to teach each other
and to listen to you.
Let us be celebratory, let us listen,
let us share our joy in you and in each other.

Prayers and invocations work best when they come from cultivated knowledge of who you invoke and of your own heart. Mabon is a holiday for gratitude—but it's okay if you don't feel magickally grateful at this time. Some years do render bad harvests. According to James Frazier, ancient Pagans used to bury god statues upside down and engage in other ritual abuses when crops were bad. Modern Pagans don't really do that—in part, because most of us live in places where bad crops look more like small paychecks and high rents but also because many Pagans believe even symbolic aggression does more harm than good. Connecting spiritually during tough times isn't about being rewarded, it's about having a conversation, even if you're not entirely sure the conversation is one-sided. Sometimes just engaging in the act of prayer is calming enough. Make offerings as you can, pray if you can, and perhaps look for gratitude in the reality that seasons pass no matter what.

RITUALS
OF
CELEBRATION

resin – spiritualization, prosperity, the mysteries of redemption, ancestors, echinacea – healing, strengthening hyssop – purification, patience, loyalty, eternal life, concentration, love myrrh – purification, protection, spirituality, Solomon's seal – exorcizing, purification, connecting to ancestors, connecting to land oak – protection, luck, health, money, fertility, Pine – healing – protection, prosperity, health, the sea Maple – love, friendship, prosperity, healing, prosperity, sleep Flowers carnation marigold – protection, healing sunflower – purity, optimism are no stones specifically associated with Mabon. However, stones or sun dials are appropriate to this holiday. Animals, totems, guiding animals in the Mabinogion that helped lead Arthur's spirit world the Blackbird – one of the guiding animals in the prosperity, men to Mabon; brings messages of other worlds, to the of the guiding animals in the Mabinogion that helped lead hunting and wisdom the Eagle – one of the guiding animals and Arthur's men to Mabon; associated with wisdom, ancient Salmon – one of the guiding animals in the Mabinogion that knowledge and past and future the Goose – associated with

$\mathcal{M}$ABON IS A time of gratitude, reflection on recent accomplishments, hard work, and planning. This is also time for personal industry—what happens now can make the difference between a comfortable winter and a harsh one. The rituals that follow are meant to help you connect with these concepts and with the balancing energy of the earth at equinox. Where the soil had heat, it now has coolness; the first frost is coming, if it hasn't arrived already. The presence of frost changes everything. As the earth's energy drifts into darkness, your own energy may turn inward. Just as it's wise to plant bulbs that need the deepest earth in fall, it's wise to seed any self-healing work or deep inner changes at this time, for gestation through the darker days to come. If you can gather a few moments alone during this busy season, use that time to take stock of what you would like to change about your inner climate. Do you want to spend less time worrying? Do you want to have a more positive outlook? Do you wish to be more discerning in your personal relationships? These desires are your ritual plan for the winter months. You can draw on the energy of Mabon to help you make these inner changes happen.

While spells focus on creating outer changes, rituals are about inner changes. They can be long or short, have companions or partners, or be performed alone. The rituals of Mabon are usually a sort of preparation for what comes next or an assessment of what came before with an eye to the known and room for the unknown difficulties of the coming winter season.

What follows here are rituals intended to celebrate the moment but also to plant deep seeds that, with nurturing through the winter, will flourish at the times in life that you need them the most. Included is a solo ritual, another for a couple, and a last one for a group to perform.

Mabon Solitary Ritual

A Mabon ritual performed alone is often a much more solemn rite than one performed in a group. It is usually also better to keep such rituals simple—the more moving parts involved, the more likely you need a spotter. There is no need to memorize this ritual. Prepare for this as if you are giving yourself a treat. Rituals should not feel like an onerous duty. To Pagans, they are acts of celebration and acknowledgment. This should produce a feeling of relaxation and a deeper connection to the Mabon season.

Purpose:

This ritual is one of simple gratitude and propitiation. In this ritual, you give offerings in the form of liquid, or libations, and by doing so you encourage a further relationship with deity and nature. Humanity has poured libations as offerings to the gods since the days of antiquity. It's simple, easy to remember, and easy to do on the spot since all it requires is liquid and sincerity. In this particular case, the ritual action is intended to attune you to the Autumn Equinox phase of the earth's cycle, when hard work is happening and just about to wrap up in time for the winter resting period. When attunement takes, you are more aware of the changing seasons and more likely to notice the subtle indicators of transition. Rather than just noticing the leaves change color, you might notice that murder of crows that gathers in your neighbor's backyard every September 4 or that extra two minutes of darkness at the end of every day.

Libations are simply liquid offerings, such as pouring out a glass of wine. There is no set size for a libation. You can spill a few drops, spill a full glass, or pour out an entire bottle. For this ritual, a finger of liquid for each pour is fine. If you have anything left at the end of ritual, it is perfectly okay to drink it in safe amounts.

Setting:

Outdoors is preferable because of less mess to clean up. Indoors can be done over a sink or tub.

Supplies:

- Smudge stick (sage, Palo Santo wood, or a frankincense incense stick) or a standard kitchen broom. If you use the smudge, you do not have to use all of it at once. You can snuff it out for future reuse.

- 5 bowls (if performing indoors)

- Wine, cider, water, or beer

- Decorations, if desired: walnuts, sunflower seeds, autumn foliage, acorns, etc.

- A tray to hold your ritual pieces

- Any tool you prefer for circle casting. While athames and wands are traditional, favorite pens are also an acceptable choice.

- One or more candles (optional)

Pre-Ritual Preparation for an Outdoor Ritual:

Wear clean, comfortable clothing that fits close to your body (a T-shirt and jeans are good for this). Prepare your tray with the liquid you plan to use for libation, whether it's water, grape juice, cider, beer, or wine. Decorate the tray with the nuts, leaves, or other symbols of Mabon that speak to you. Take your tray outside and place it in a spot where you can easily walk all the way around it without bumping into anything. Use your smudge stick or a broom to clear the sacred space of lingering energies. If smudging, light your bundle or stick and walk clockwise around your ritual space, waving up and down, telling the smoke to cleanse the air and land of all energies that conflict with your intentions. Walk from north to south and then, forming a cross, do the same from east to west. Make sure you wave the smudge stick up and down, getting above your head and below your knees as you go. Imagine the space getting brighter, as though a patch of sunlight is shining on it.

You might want to add a spell or chant element to the smudging. One such chant you can use is:

> *Cloud of smoke borne of sagebrush,*
> *bring this space to a quiet hush;*
> *scrub it of all pain and meanness,*
> *let these rites go forward clean.*

Give yourself about two feet more space than you think you need. Snuff out the sage on the ground if you can do so without risk of starting a fire. Otherwise, pour a little water over it and set it down in a place it can dry safely. Place the bundle on the tray and then take a few moments to sit down on the ground; feel the air on your skin, how the sky overhead affects your mood, and the changes you have witnessed from the previous Mabon to this one. Take several deep breaths. Start the ritual once you feel relaxed.

Pre-Ritual Preparation for an Indoor Ritual:

If sweeping with the broom in lieu of smudging, again go clockwise around the circle, stating, "I sweep out any energies that conflict with my intentions." If you wish a more intensive chant, as you sweep, chant:

> *Cleanse the air and free the dirt,*
> *move out of here what lays inert.*
> *Whip out all conflicts, dust up disruptors;*
> *let peace reconstruct this space!*

Once you have completed smudging and put away your cleansing tool, place five bowls in your designated sacred space to catch the libations—one in each of the cardinal directions and the fifth bowl on a tray in the center of your space. Surround that bowl with autumn foliage, acorns, walnuts, and sunflower seeds.

Speaking out loud during ritual may feel especially silly when you practice alone. It can also help you set your own mind for the work ahead—and for most practitioners it really does help better direct the thrust and mood. In addition, many Pagans theorize that their gods are not omnipotent; they have to hear you say something to know what you're thinking.

The Ritual:

Cast a circle by saying:

> *At Autumn Equinox, I name this place*
> *a sacred time and sacred space.*
> *Within it I now give my thanks,*
> *with protection granted by God/ess grace!*
> *The north grants ground to walk upon.*
> *The east grants winds that gyrate.*
> *The south grants fire so we live on.*
> *The west grants fluids to sate us.*

At this point, take one swig from the drink container. This tradition demonstrates that the beverage is safe for those to whom it is offered.

It is time for the invocation. Say:

Hail to the God/ess, Great Mother Eternal,
I salute you in your giving;
I condole you in your grief.

Pour a libation from the bottle into the center bowl. Then say:

In gratitude, in love,
I give thanks to you.

You may wish to light a candle or incense representing the God/ess. Instead, you can simply raise your hands heavenward and say:

In your grief, in your sorrow,
I give love to you.
So mote it be!

Then say:

Hail to the God, Great Father Incarnate,
I salute you for your sacrifices.
I speak your praises when you are gone from us!

Pour libation into the center bowl, then say:

In your death, I speak my grief.
In your memory, I bring you to life.
So mote it be!

Go to the northern bowl or to the northernmost point of the circle:

Hail to the north, where the dark of the earth lives.
I pour this in gratitude for the food that springs from soil!

Pour libation in the northern bowl. Then go to the eastern bowl or to the easternmost point of the circle and say:

Hail to the east, where sunrise brings the winds of the day,
I pour this in gratitude for the movements of pollen!

Pour libation in the eastern bowl. Then, go to the southern bowl or to the southernmost point of the circle and say:

Hail to the south, where noonday speeds all growth.
I pour this in gratitude for the nourishment of sunlight!

Pour libation into the southern bowl, then go to the western bowl or to the westernmost point of the circle and say:

Hail to the west, where in twilight the green drinks deep.
I pour this in gratitude for the wet that swells seed and bud!

Pour libation into the eastern bowl. Return to the center bowl and pour any remaining libation in it. Then say:

Hail to the Goddes! Hail to the God!
I give thanks for good harvest
and thanks for all good.
So mote it be!

Take a few moments to meditate, whether standing or sitting. Imagine a seed in the earth swelling until a shoot of green bursts forth. See that green stripe expand until it becomes a plant. Make note of the plant you see to learn about it over the winter. Visualize that plant brightening, flowering, and eventually going to seed until it is brown and felled to the earth. Notice that at the end of the cycle, the seed is blown by the wind to new ground. At the end of the ritual, take note of the corner you "saw" the seed emerge. The quarter of the circle that held your vision shows where the work of your next harvest lies.

At the end of this meditation, you may wish to nod or make other acknowledgments to the deities and elements. To say farewell, say:

With love, I depart from you, precious Goddess.
With love, I depart from you, sacred God.
I carry with me gratitude for the life on earth you have given.

To open the circle, walk counterclockwise with your arm extended and say:

Water flows back to the west.
Southern fires flicker then rest.
Eastern breezes cool the storm.
North rests now in quiet calm.
At equinox the light now fades,
here is now more night than it is day.
In gratitude I make my way
with harvest at hand into winter's sway.

After the circle is open, clean up your sacred space. If you did the ritual indoors, it is acceptable to pour the libations on the ground outside your house or down a sink drain. If outdoors, gather up any remaining material on your tray and take it away—into your house, in your car, etc. After this ritual, enjoy a hearty meal that includes a mix of grains, vegetables, and fruits to represent the harvest.

Mabon Ritual for a Couple

For those who subscribe to the mythos of the dying god, the meaning of Mabon for couples is a challenge; it is about facing the reality that one day you will lose one another. While loss has become more ambiguous these days—divorce, serious illness, and emotional distance loom larger in our collective consciousness—the possibility of death remains, hidden behind the rest.

The couple need not be a man and a woman, but every couple should understand the laws of nature inherent in the Autumn Equinox holiday symbolism. Embedded in even the old Harvest Home celebrations was an acknowledgment that the harvest required two parts to happen—fertility and pollination. Because it centered on old fertility cults, it often required specific genders for specific roles. The Lord and Lady of the Manor usually represented the generating partners in the festivities. However, the other lord and lady mentioned in chapter 1—the two head reapers—paired two men but could be any gender configuration at all. In both cases, the Lord and Lady needed one another. One, so that life could be, the other so that work and life could continue when one had to go conduct business on the household or worker's behalf. Perhaps each could have survived without the other, but it was unlikely that one could thrive without the other.

Today our interdependence on partners is more subtle. We may literally conceive, but often enough even conception is metaphorical in nature. One person inspires the other to look for new creative solutions to life's problems, comforts the other during life's difficulties, or simply shares the burden of household life and work. Again, that other person may not be technically necessary for survival, but a healthy, close relationship still improves our chances for a long and healthy life. Take a moment to honor this. Life is always easier when someone is around to share the load.

Purpose:

This ritual is a way for partners to take time out to honor one another. In addition to being thankful for the harvest bounty, this is a way to show each person that gratitude for the other. If it's been a difficult year, this is a good way to acknowledge each other as partners and as a team, to help fortify one another for the challenges of the coming winter.

Setting:

Perform this ritual outside or inside, at any time of day when you can avoid interruption—a city park, a backyard, a living room floor, or, in a pinch, a parking lot near a storm drain will do.

Supplies:

- A bowl of water
- Two clean washcloths
- Two clean hand towels
- Two letters: one by each person to his/her partner
- A small plate of food—bread, fruit, cheese, etc.
- A bottle of any beverage—water, wine, cider, etc. Plan to drink straight from the bottle or to share a single glass if you wish to pour out.
- A picnic blanket (optional)
- A wand, athame, or similar item to use for circle casting

Pre-Ritual Preparation

Write a heartfelt letter to your partner. The choice of paper and pen doesn't matter; be simple with a ballpoint pen, fanciful with typed fonts, or magickal with quill and ink. Make a list of everything you are grateful for in that person, from the trivial to the gigantic. Carry it close to your heart until called to produce it in the ritual. (You may want to fasten it inside your shirt with a safety pin.)

Each person should take a bath or shower and change into loose, comfortable clothing—this ritual should be relaxed. Go barefoot if possible.

Assemble the plate of food with small items you can both safely eat. Fresh, just harvested foods are ideal; whatever is easily available to you is very good. Put down the picnic blanket (if you have it). In the center, place the bowl of water, washcloths, and towels on one side. On the other side, set the plate of food and the beverage (and glass for pouring, if desired).

Decide between you who casts a circle, calls the quarters, and makes the first move once the space is established. One partner should cast the circle and the other call the quarters. If you need to, flip a coin.

The Ritual:

The first partner performs a circle casting, walking deosil (clockwise), while saying:

> *Circle, full circle we come to this space,*
> *in a time without time,*
> *in this place between places.*
> *Together we are safe both outside and in,*
> *as we share heart-to-heart what lies deep within.*

Then the second partner performs quarter calls by saying:

> *Hail to the east, may we speak our truths well!*
> *Hail to the south, may we feel true warmth for one another!*

Hail to the west, may we flow well with one another!
Hail to the north, may we live together in trust!
So mote it be!

Settle yourselves on the blanket across from each another, with the bowl of water and the plate of food between you. Gaze into each other's eyes for a full minute. Meditate on the person before you, the meaning he or she has to you, and what you see inside that person. First, one partner should pick up a washcloth, dip it in the water, wring it out, and then proceed to wash his or her partner's hands and feet. Be gentle and thorough. When done, dry off and set the cloths away from the blanket.

Take the letter out from where you've been keeping it. Read it to your partner. Take your time. When finished, hold a moment of silence. Then the partner who has not yet read should reciprocate the process, washing the hands and feet, drying them, and reading his or her letter of gratitude.

Once you have completed these actions, the partner that washed first should set the bowl of water and cloths outside the immediate ritual area. The other partner should then pick up the plate of food and gently feed a bite to the other partner, saying: *May you never hunger*. The partner just fed should in turn feed his/her partner, and say: *May you never hunger*. The partner who just ate should open the beverage bottle and pour it into the glass, offering it and saying, *May you never thirst*. The partner who just received should offer it back, also saying: *May you never thirst*.

Finish the plate of food and take a few more moments to enjoy one another's company. Tuck the letters away someplace safe to read in times when you most need or miss one another.

Release the quarters and close the circle. After this, take the bowl of water and pour it in the soil, saying, *All in this water, come to good again*. (If in the parking lot, pour it down the storm drain saying the same thing.) Clean up, head home, throw the wet cloth in the laundry, and wash the plates. Enjoy a quiet evening together.

Mabon Ritual for a Group

This is a ritual for a group. It will require someone to assign parts. Because it is a sabbat feast, prepare all the food before the ritual begins. Those handling the feast part of the festivities will have enough to do! A person with good organization skills should divide the work so that each participant only has one job. This can include parts of the ritual, who takes kitchen duty, and who leads the ritual. You may want to print copies of the ritual ahead of time as well; most people do not have time for memorizing long passages.

Purpose:

This ritual connects its participants with the strange combination of pride, grief, loss, and gratitude that Mabon brings forth. It should affirm the links of the group to one another, helping them recognize one another as part of a functional community while also honoring and giving thanks for the sacrifice of the dying god. Like Harvest Home, the entire group will have different, equally important roles; those in the ritual will represent the reapers and the Lord and Lady of the Manor. Those preparing the feast represent the village/greater community and handling the business of life while the workers are in the field.

Setting:

Outside—a picnic shelter is ideal for this type of ritual

Supplies:

- An effigy made of wheat or other harvested plants
- Wreaths made of flowers that fit atop a person's head; one for each ritual participant, if possible
- A bell
- Libations, such as cider, wine, juices, or olive oil
- A tray, table, or flat board to use as an altar
- A jar containing a handful of soil from each participant's garden; potting soil also works

- A box that fits the effigy as closely as possible
- Binders or cheat sheets/index card containing relevant parts of this ritual for participants
- Brown or black candles
- Hurricane lamps or similar wind-shelter candleholders
- A silly hat or paper crown for the "harvest lord" during the feast

Pre-Ritual Preparation:

Before beginning, divide ritual roles. Draw from a hat (or use a similar random method) to determine who is in the ritual and who conducts the feast. At least three group members should handle the feast.

Those planning the feast should be given at least a week to coordinate details, including a call to the entire group for potluck dishes, etc. Those handling the feast should also plan for music and games.

On the day of the ritual, set up a clean altar space. The altar should be as clear as possible. The bulk of the space should go to housing the box for the effigy. Additional space should be set aside for libation bowls or simple representations of the God and Goddess. On either side of the effigy, place candles that are inside hurricane lamps or similar candleholders that can block wind.

Designate a table outside the circle for the feast. You may also collect canned goods and personal items for donation to a local food shelf; place a box at the end of the table for this purpose. Decorate the edges of the table with autumn leaves, acorns, and tablecloths in browns, reds, yellows, oranges, and greens. Also, add pictures or figures of geese and pigs.

Assign all participants a specific cleanup task ahead of time.

Pre-Ritual Meditation

One person should read this guided meditation to the entire group before splitting off into the ritual circle and the feast preparation circle. Have everyone who is able sit on the ground or on a picnic bench. Then begin the meditation:

Take three deep breaths. (Pause) Feel the air around you on your skin. Take off your shoes, if able. Feel the ground against your feet, the way it presses up to you as you press your feet down against it. Listen to what's going on around you—wind blowing, other people shouting, laughing, or talking, and traffic roaring in the distance. Everything you hear is a part of the life of the land. You are a part of the life of the land. Take a moment to breathe that into you. (Pause) Feel the pulse of the land beneath your feet. Feel how it reaches up and pulses into you. Take a moment to feel how it pulses into the people next to and around you. Take a moment to imagine how a plant might feel that pulse. (Pause)

Now, picture yourself standing in the middle of a wheat field. Each sheaf reaches toward the sky —these stalks are gigantic, at least a foot taller than the tallest among us. You have a row to yourself. Through the pulse of the earth, feel your companions standing in the other rows.

A wind blows through the wheat, causing a ripple of grain to run through the field like a wave. You see it as one stalk knocking into another before bending back upright. In the wind, you hear a whispering: "This is how it feels, this is how it feels."

Impressions come to you of the seed buried in the earth. You feel hot and moist and dark, the sense of sweat a reassurance of life. Each drop of moisture, each touch of pleasant warmth makes you feel more expansive until, at last, you burst free, raising your body up to meet the sun.

In this space, reaching for the sun, you feel vulnerable. Loving warmth becomes too hot, too close, and the cooling rain helps you breath in and out according to that subterranean beat that regulates you. Then the rain keeps pouring—more than you can drink. You start to feel your roots loosen and again there is that sense of vulnerability. Who do you call to for protection? Suddenly the rain stops. You find you have grown stronger. When wind blows, you bend but do not break. When rain comes, you tighten your roots against the soil and drink deep, raising it to your crown, your crown always reaching toward the solar rays.

One day, you find yourself preoccupied—you have grown as much as you can, and now you find yourself extending, expanding. Your body extends and changes and, in a burst of relief, you drop seeds from your stalks, sweet children stemming from you that will, in an ecstasy of heat and moisture, someday burst from the ground. You feel the satisfaction of having finished. Then, you feel just a little less heat from the sun—just a little more rain. You are tired and wish to rest. Rather than stand tall, you want to lie flat on the field as the ground cools and tightens under the burden of frost. This is as it should be. (Pause)

Come back to yourself, standing in the wheat fields. Now the wheat is lying flat on the ground. The harvest came, and reapers moved by you as you communed with the grain. You can see one another, standing in the wheat rows, you can feel that sense of completion, the hard work that went to making this field flat, and yet more hard work is to come in converting it to things needed to survive the winter. From

somewhere beneath the stalks you hear a voice whispering,
"Remember this feeling."

Take a moment to pause and ask, "Who are you?" Take
a moment to let the Mother of the Grain tell you who she is
to you. (Pause)

Come back to where you began in time and space. Wiggle
your fingers and toes, take a big, deep, refreshing breath, and
open your eyes. You are ready to begin this ritual.

Once members complete the meditation before the ritual
and/or a sweeping of the circle, the ritual may begin.

The Ritual:

The Priest/ess casts the circle, saying:

Circle, full circle, we come to this point
where the harvest is waning though our spirits are buoyant.
Into this circle, we call those who labor.
Once we give thanks, a blessed feast we will savor—
with thanks and through grace, we encircle this place
to give thanks for the harvest and give due to the Fates!

A member of the group calls to the east, saying:

Hail to the east, to the winds that have blessed us!
Be gentle of breeze and gentle of gust—
it is by your currents that the seeds have their thrust!

A member of the group calls to the south, saying:

Hail to the south, to the warm that does linger.
Keep us so sweetly with wood and with cinder—
it is by your passion that we turn seed to timber!

A member of the group calls to the west, saying:

Hail to the west, to the waters and wet!
Give moisture to us and nourish the rest—
it is by your succor and sweat that we give our respect!

A member of the group calls to the north, saying:

Hail to the north, to the earth turned and tilled,
give to us the place where our seed may be spilled—
it is by your mercy that we have a future to build!

The Priest/ess invokes the Goddess, saying:

Hail to the Goddess, Great Mother and Lover,
she who guides us from hot work to winter slumber.
In your grief do you lead us, in your joy we do rise,
as your husband lays dying, we give thanks
for the wheat, corn, and rye!

Pour a libation of apple cider, red wine, juice, or honey. Then, the assisting Priest/ess invokes the God, saying:

Hail to the God, Green Man of the soil,
we have followed you each season to know where to toil.
We mourn you, we grieve you, we lay you to rest—
a great king you are and you gave us your best.
We thank you, we mourn you, we raise our hands to the sky;
you have allowed us this living all that you may die.

Pour a libation of beer and honey and light a brown or black candle to indicate fertility and sorrow. The Priest/ess moves to stand before the effigy, facing the west. He or she anoints it with honey and olive oil, saying,

We thank you, Lord of the Harvest, Divine King of the Land.
In the moment of your dying,
let us thank you for the good you have brought us.

He/she moves to the middle of the circle, where the assisting priest/ess joins him/her. The Priest/ess that invoked the Goddess says:

Come forth, lord and lady of the reapers!

Two members of the group, both wearing garlands on their heads, act as pallbearers, hoisting the effigy from the table and walking it around the circle. They stop together before each member present. Each person confronted thanks the effigy for the good things that happened that year, for lessons learned, and for difficulties survived. They may ask the king also to bring words of blessing to loved ones now passed beyond the veil. If desired, letters of petition or small offerings may be tucked inside the coffin.

As each person gives his or her personal thanks, the others in the circle should begin a solemn chant. This helps keep attention to the ritual itself and allows those speaking to the effigy some modicum of privacy. One such chant might be:

Hail to the King of the dying light,
well earned is your rest at autumn tide.
Thoughts of your grace at summer's height
will give strength to us through the winter.

When the circumambulation has finished, the pallbearers should set the effigy down at the feet of the two Priest/esses in the center of the circle, remove the wreaths from their heads, and confer them to those at the center of the circle, saying:

Gracious Lady and Gracious Lord of this land, we crown you.
You are that which the harvest has given us.

The Priest/ess that invoked the Goddess rings a bell as the Priest/ess that invoked the God announces,

This day I invite you, all who have labored, to break bread with me!

The attendees should raise a cheer. The Priest/ess should then set the effigy back on the table. The Goddess-invoking Priest/ess should sprinkle a handful of dirt over the figure, saying:

Go to the earth, O Dying God. The grounds will freeze, and we will grieve. We will greet your return in the spring with great joy!

The accompanying Priest/ess says:

This night will be a gracious feast; in it, we remember him who gave us all in life that we call sweet.

Everyone: *Blessed be.*

The Priest/ess that performed the first invocation pours a final libation to the God and Goddess on the ground, saying:

> *Blessed Lady, our thoughts are with you*
> *as we go into the dark of the year,*
> *as you go into the dark of the earth.*
> *Be welcome at our feast this night;*
> *our solemnities are done!*
> *Blessed be!*

The assisting priest/ess then steps up, taking the bottle from the first priest/ess and pours a libation, saying:

> *Blessed Harvest Lord, we salute you*
> *and give great thanks for your sacrifice.*
> *It is by your body*
> *that we may live*
> *and live again.*
> *Be welcome at our feast this night;*
> *it is in your honor we have it!*
> *Blessed be!*

The Priest/esses (Lord and Lady of the Land) step back into the circle as those who called the original quarters resume their original places at each quarter point in the circle.

The person who called to the north raises his/her arms and says:

> To the north! The soil now may rest, frozen in the
> Lady's breast. We shall see you in the spring
> when you render us the young new king!
> Farewell!
> So mote it be!

The person who called to the west raises his/her arms and says:

> To the west! We watch the streams stop their flow
> and await your rain that turns to snow.
> Blanket us in your cold, while deep in the earth the new god grows.
> Farewell!
> So mote it be!

The person who called to the south raises his/her arms and says:

> To the south! We move our fires from field to hearth,
> gathering embers close to our hearts.

In light is hope and comfort given—
in darkest days we come to you, our spark within.
Farewell!
So mote it be!

The person who called to the east raises his/her arms and says:

To the east! The breezes must give way
to gales that bring the coldest streams of air.
Beneath your wind the earth will pale,
and we will face what we must bear.
Farewell!
So mote it be!

The Priest/ess who cast the circle steps to the edge of the circle in the north and moves widdershins (counterclockwise) to open the circle, saying:

The circle cast this autumn night
has filled with solemnity and delight;
we take it to bless the harvest table:
Come ye, come ye all who are able!
So mote it be!

Retire to the feast that features as much garden/homemade fare as possible.

While those performing in the circle enacted the ritual role of the reapers, those preparing the feast will be enacting the ritual role of the villagers. The ritual of meal preparation is a common one. Most adults know how to set a table and cook for a guest. Meals for large groups usually only happen on holidays. As those who have cooked an American Thanksgiving dinner know, there is just as much preparation and work in cooking a feast as there is in conducting a ritual.

Do what you need to clean and prepare the food, add any decorations to the table you can assemble from what you find in the space around you. After all is prepared, chant a blessing together over the meal:

Corn mother, grain mother, Demeter, Ceres,
hail to you!
Great mother, blessed mother,
bless this food as we praise you!

While people are eating, one of those who prepared the feast should don the silly hat and wander around the table, collecting coins to go to the food shelf or to raise funds for the next ritual. Once finished, the "harvest lord" should raise a toast to the group, highlighting the themes of gratitude and loss and mentioning accomplishments of other group members.

During cleanup, someone should put on music so that people may start dancing or chatting once they finish their tasks. A game of horseshoes—the closest equivalent to the wheat-felling games of Harvest Home—is an appropriate way to end the celebration. Any children in attendance can go collect acorns and nuts, in keeping with the old nutting traditions. Use the nuts in crafts and spellwork for the coming Samhain season.

CORRESPONDENCES
FOR
MABON

resin – purification, prosperity, the mysteries of autumn eq
ancestors, echinacea – healing, strengthening hyssop – purifica
tion, patience, loyalty, eternal life, concentration, love myrrh
purification, protection, spirituality, Solomon's seal – exor
ing, purification, connecting to ancestors, connecting to land y
h – protection, luck, health, money, fertility, Pine – healing
– protection, prosperity, health, the sea Maple – love, friend
m, prosperity, healing, prosperity, sleep Flowers carnation
marigold – protection, healing sunflower – purity, optimism
e no stones specifically associated with Mabon. However, se
or sun disks are appropriate to this holiday. Animals, tote
iding animals in the Mabinogion that helped lead Arthur's
it world the Blackbird – one of the guiding animals in the
perity, men to Mabon; brings messages of other worlds to t
of the guiding animals in the Mabinogion that helped lead
hunting and wisdom the Eagle – one of the guiding animals
and Arthur's men to Mabon; associated with wisdom, insig
fison – one of the guiding animals in the Mabinogion that
of knowledge and past and future the Sa

Spiritual Focus and Key Words

Accomplishment

balance

death

equality

equilibrium

goals

gratitude

grief

healing

love

preparation

sharing

success

Magickal Focus

Agriculture

community

family harmony
grounding
honor
planning
public safety
wisdom

Suggested Workings
Concentration and study
preparation
transition

Astrological Timing and Associated Planets
Astronomical equinox marking the waning point of the sun;
Sun enters 0 degrees of Libra in the Northern Hemisphere,
Sun at 0 degrees of Libra in the Southern Hemisphere. The
alignment of planets changes from year to year.

Archetypes
FEMALE
The Grieving Widow
Harvest Lady
Harvest Queen

Kern Baby
the Warrior Woman

The Divine King
the Dying God
the Harvest Lord
the Warrior Man

Deities and Heroes

GODDESSES
Demeter (Greek)
Epona (Celtic)
Ereshkigal (Sumerian)
Inanna (Sumerian)
Juno (Roman)
Minerva (Roman)
Modron (Celtic)
the Muses (Greek)
Persephone (Greek)
Osun (Yoruba)
Yemaya (Yoruba)
Oya (Yoruba)

GODS

Apollo (Greek)

Dionysus (Greek)

Green Man (Celtic)

Hermes (Greek)

Jupiter (Roman)

Mabon (Celtic)

Thor (Norse)

Thoth (Egyptian)

Vulcan (Roman)

Colors

Brown: Balance, family, grounding, hearth, home, stability

Green: Fertility, generosity, growth, harmony, healing, love, rebirth

Orange: Action, balance, kindness, luck, optimism, warmth

Red: Action, changes, fertility, passion, protection, wisdom

Yellow: Creativity, happiness, light, optimism

Herbs

Acorns: Fertility, health, luck, money, protection

Bay: Courage, dedication to Apollo, valor, victory

Benzoin resin: Balance, concentration, the Mysteries of Autumn Equinox, prosperity, purification

Echinacea: Healing, strengthening

Hyssop: Healing, purification

Ivy: Attachment, attraction, love, omens, protection

Myrrh: Healing, purification

Sage: Protection, purification, spirituality

Solomon's seal: Exorcism, protection, purification

Tobacco: Connecting to ancestors, connecting to land, healing, purification

Yarrow: Friendship, healing, marriage

Trees

Ash: Health, prosperity, protection

Elder: Healing, prosperity, sleep

Maple: Abundance, balance, love, prosperity

Oak: Fertility, health, luck, money, protection

Flowers

Carnation: Calm, healing, well-being

Chrysanthemum: Cheerfulness

Marigold: Healing, protection

Sunflower: Spirituality, wisdom

Crystals and Stones

Amber: Eternal love, protection, spirituality

Golden topaz: Health, protection, wisdom

Hematite: Grounding, healing

Metals

Antimony: Protection

Gold: Prosperity, the sun

Iron: Protection from fairies

Animals, Totems, and Mythical Creatures

The Blackbird: One of the guiding animals in the Mabinogion that helped lead Arthur's men to Mabon; brings messages from other worlds to those in this one

the Eagle: One of the guiding animals in the Mabinogion that helped lead Arthur's men to Mabon; associated with wisdom, insight, and knowledge

the Goose: Geese were often raised and then served at the harvest meal; associated with transition

horses: the Scottish had riding competitions around the Autumn Equinox

the Owl: One of the guiding animals in the Mabinogion that helped lead Arthur's men to Mabon; associated with Athena, hunting, and wisdom

the Salmon: One of the guiding animals in the Mabinogion that helped lead Arthur's men to Mabon; wisdom and knowledge of past and future

squirrels: Behavior of the animals represents the preparation for harvest; also harvest nuts, making them competition at Roodmas

the Stag: One of the guiding animals in the Mabinogion that helped lead Arthur's men to Mabon; represents assistance / presence of the ancestors / spirit world

Scents for Oils, Incense, Potpourri, or Just Floating in the Air

Aloe

benzoin

burning leaves

cinnamon

cedar

clove

frankincense

myrrh

pine

Tarot keys

The Empress

the Hanged Man

Wheel of Fortune

the World

Symbols and Tools

Cornucopias and baskets: Symbolizing the abundant harvest

Effigies and scarecrows: Symbolizing the dying god and also the protector of the fields

Garlands and wreaths: Symbolizing the Lord and Lady at
  Autumnal Equinox
Scythes, bolines, and sickles: Symbolizing death and the work of
  the harvest

Foods

Apples

barley

bread

carrots

corn

gourds

grapes

melons

nuts

oats

onions

potatoes

rye

wheat

Drinks

Beer

cider

mead

water

wine

Activities and Traditions of Practice
Communal feasting (corn roasts, barbecues, shared dinners)
effigy burning
dancing
dunk tank games
music
parades/processionals
target games

Acts of Service
Food drives
nursing home and hospice visits
park and highway cleanups
public school service and booster projects
veterans' care

Alternate Names for Mabon in Other Pagan Traditions
Aequinoctium Auctumnale (Hellenic, celebrates agriculture and end of military campaign season)
Alban Elfed (Druid, celebrates final harvest and balance of light and dark)
Equinozio di Autunno (Stregha)

Feast of Avalon (Welsh Celtic)

Meán Fómhair (Gaelic, "middle of autumn" and modern Irish word for September)

Holidays or Traditions Occurring During Mabon in the Northern Hemisphere:

RELIGIOUS

Ampelia (Hellenic, honoring harvest and sacrifice, August 19)

Vinalia (Nova Romans, celebrating wine harvest, August 19)

Eleusinian Mysteries (Hellenic, approximately September 11–20)

Feast of Jupiter, Juno, Minerva (Nova Romans, September 13)

Boedromion (Hellenic festival honoring the dead, September 19)

Harvest Home (Scottish Celts, celebrating final harvest around the end of autumn)

Michaelmas (Catholic Christian, honoring archangel Michael, strength of will, September 29)

Mimneskia (Hellenic, Roman suppression of the Bacchanalia, October 7)

Winter Finding (Heathen / Norse, from equinox to October 15)

SECULAR

Second Harvest Festival (Autumn Equinox in mid-September)

Thanksgiving (Last Thursday in November in United States)

Holidays or Traditions Occurring During Mabon in the Southern Hemisphere:

RELIGIOUS

Dionysus or Bacchus Day (Greco Roman, March 16–17)

Annunciation of the Blessed Virgin Mary or Lady Day (Catholic, March 25)

Palm Sunday (Christian, the Sunday before Easter)

Good Friday (Christian, the Friday before Easter)

Easter (Christian, the first Sunday after the first full moon after the Spring Equinox)

Passover (Jewish, fifteenth day of Nisan, which begins on the night of the full moon after the northern Vernal Equinox)

SECULAR

St. Patrick's Day (while originally the Catholic Feast Day of a Saint, it is celebrated more as a secular holiday of Irish culture around the world, March 17)

FURTHER
READING

Books

Davies, Sioned. *The Mabinogion*. London: Oxford University Press, 2008.

Dugan, Ellen. *Autumn Equinox: The Enchantment of Mabon*. St. Paul, MN: Llewellyn Publications, 2005.

Kelly, Aidan. *Inventing Witchcraft: A Case Study in the Creation of a New Religion*. Leicestershire, England: Thoth Publications, 2007.

———. *Religious Holidays and Calendars: An Encyclopedic Handbook*. Aston, PA: Omnigraphics, 1993.

O'Gaea, Ashleen. *Celebrating the Seasons of Life: Beltane to Mabon*. Pompton Plains, NJ: Career Press, 2008.

Wasson, R. Gordon. *The Road to Eleusis: Unveiling the Secret Mysteries*. Berkeley, CA: North Atlantic Books, 2008.

Online

Bulfinch, Thomas. *Bulfinch's Mythology*. Internet Sacred Text Archive, 1855. http://www.sacred-texts.com/cla/bulf/.

Colum, Padraic. *Orpheus: Myths of the World*. Internet Sacred Text Archive, 1930. http://www.sacred-texts.com/etc/omw/index.htm.

Hunt, J. M. "The Wanderings of Dionysus." *Greek Mythology*. http://edweb.sdsu.edu/people/bdodge/scaffold/gg/wanderDionysus.html.

BIBLIOGRAPHY

Books

Campbell, John Gregerson. *Witchcraft and Second Sight in the Highland & Islands of Scotland: Tales & Traditions Collected Entirely from Oral Sources*. Glasgow: James MacLehose & Sons, 1902.

Chambers, Robert. *The Book of Days: A Miscellany of Popular Antiquities in Connection with the Calendar, Including Anecdote, Biography, History, Curiosities of Literature and Oddities of Life and Human Character*. London and Edinburgh: W & R Chambers, 1862.

Dalyell, John Graham. *The Darker Superstitions of Scotland*. Edinburgh: Waugh and Innes, 1835.

Daniels, Cora Linn Morrison, and Charles McLellan Stevens, eds. *Encyclopaedia of Superstitions, Folklore, and the Occult Sciences of the World*. Vol. 3. Chicago: J. H. Yewdale & Sons, 1908.

Folkard, Richard. *Plant Lore, Legends, and Lyrics*. London: Sampson Low, Marston, Searle, and Rivington, 1884.

Goldsmith, Milton. *Signs, Omens and Superstitions*. New York: George Sully and Company, 1918.

Gomme, George Laurence. *Archaeological Review*. Vol. 2. London: D. Nutt, 1889.

Hastings, James. *Encyclopedia of Religion & Ethics*. Vol. VI. Edinburgh: T & T Clark, 1914.

Hughes, Kristoffer. *The Book of Celtic Magic: Transformative Teachings from the Cauldron of Awen*. Woodbury, MN: Llewellyn Publications, 2014.

Mylonas, George E. *Eleusis and the Eleusinian Mysteries*. Princeton, NJ: Princeton University Press, 1962.

Smith, Horace. *Festivals, Games, and Amusements*. New York: Harper & Brothers, 1831.

Warren, Nathan B. *The Holidays: Christmas, Easter, Whitsuntide, together with the May-Day, Midsummer, and Harvest-Home Festivals*. Troy, NY: H. B. Nims & Company, 1876.

Online

Artisson, Robin. "The Differences in Traditional Witchcraft and Neo-Pagan Witchcraft, or Wicca." Accessed June 10, 2014. http://www.paganlore.com/witchcraft_vs_wicca.aspx.

Bonewits, Isaac. "Defining Paganism: Paleo-, Meso-, and Neo-." *Neopagan.net*. Accessed June 30, 2014. http://www.neopagan.net/PaganDefs.html.

Crew's Nest. "Harvest Festival UK." Accessed February 27, 2014. http://www.crewsnest.vispa.com/thanksgivingUK.htm.

The Ecole Initiative. "The Eleusinian Mysteries." Accessed June 30, 2014. http://www.bsu.edu/classes/magrath/305s01/demeter/eleusis.html.

Encyclopedia Britannica Online. "Harvest Home." Accessed February 17, 2014. http://www.britannica.com/EBchecked/topic/256338/Harvest-Home.

Fares, Aymen. "Stregheria—Basic Beliefs." Spiritual.com.au. Accessed October 28, 2014. http://www.spiritual.com.au/2011/07/stregheria-basic-beliefs/.

Fish Eaters. "Feast of St.Michael (Michaelmas)." Accessed May 26, 2014. http://www.fisheaters.com/customstimeafterpentecost10.html.

Flippo, Hyde. "Erntedankfest: Thanksgiving in Germany." *About.com*. Accessed June 30, 2014. http://german.about .com/cs/culture/a/erntedankf.htm.

Foreman, A. Z. "Poems Found in Translation: Saint John of the Cross: The Dark Night of the Soul (From Spanish)." http://poemsintranslation.blogspot.com/2009/09 /saint-john-of-cross-dark-night-of-soul.html.

Frazer, James. *The Golden Bough*. "Chapter 29. The Myth of Adonis." Internet Sacred Text Archive, 1922. http://www.sacred-texts.com/pag/frazer/gb02900.htm.

Guest, Charlotte. *The Mabinogion*. "Kilhwch and Olwen." Internet Sacred Text Archive, 1877. http://www.sacred-texts .com/neu/celt/mab/mab16.htm.

Harrison, Jane. *Myths of Greece and Rome*. "Athena." Internet Sacred Text Archive, 1928. http://www.sacred-texts.com/cla /mgr/mgr06.htm.

Kelly, Aidan. Interview with Aidan Kelly October 13, 2013.

Knowlson, T. Sharper. *The Origins of Popular Superstitions and Customs: Days and Seasons*. "(22) Harvest Home—The Kern Baby." Internet Sacred Text Archive, 1910. http://www.sacred-texts.com/neu/eng/osc/osc25.htm.

Mackenzie, Donald. *Egyptian Myth and Legend*. "Chapter II: The Tragedy of Osiris." Internet Sacred Text Archive, 1907. http://www.sacred-texts.com/egy/eml/eml05.htm.

Moore, A. W. *The Folk-Lore of the Isle of Man.* "Chapter VI. Customs and Superstitions Connected with the Seasons." Internet Sacred Text Archive, 1891. http://www.sacred-texts.com/neu/celt/fim/fim09.htm.

Museum Syndicate. "Corn Mummy in the Rosicrucian Museum." Accessed June 30, 2014. http://www.museumsyndicate.com/item.hp?item=54349.

Nichols, Mike. "Harvest Home." *The Witches' Sabbats.* http://www.witchessabbats.com/index.php?option=com_content&view=article&id=17&Itemid=28.

OFEST. "The History of Oktoberfest." Accessed March 3, 2014. http://www.ofest.com/history.html.

Order of Bards and Druids. "Autumn Equinox—Alban Elfed." Accessed June 10, 2014. http://www.druidry.org/druid-way/teaching-and-practice/druid-festivals/autumn-equinox-alban-elfed.

Pagan Pride. "About Pagan Pride." *Pagan Pride.* http://www.paganpride.org.uk/Pagan_Pride-UK-About_Pagan_Pride-2.php.

Perotta, Andrew. "The Feast of St. Michael's—History of the Fest of St. Michael's." Accessed May 25, 2014. http://www.feastofstmichael.com/history.html.

Polish Toledo. "Dozynki—Polish Harvest Festival." *PolishToledo.com.* http://www.polishtoledo.com/dozynki01.htm.

Reform Judaism. "Rosh HaShanah." *ReformJudiasm.org*. Accessed October 28, 2014. http://www.reformjudaism.org/jewish-holidays/rosh-hashanah.

———. "Sukkot—Feast of Booths." *ReformJudiasim.org*. Accessed June 10, 2014. http://www.reformjudaism.org/jewish-holidays/sukkot.

———. "Yom Kippur—Day of Atonement." *ReformJudaism.org*. Accessed June 10, 2014. http://www.reformjudaism.org/jewish-holidays/yom-kippur-day-atonement.

Rich, Tracey R. "Jewish Calendar." *Judaism 101*. Accessed October 28, 2014. http://www.jewfaq.org/calendar.htm.

Robinson, B. A. "Asatru: Norse Heathenism." *ReligiousTolerance.org*. Accessed October 28, 2014. http://www.religioustolerance.org/asatru.htm.

Springwolf. "The History of Mabon—The Feast of Avalon." *Springwolf Reflections*. Accessed June 30, 2014. http://springwolf.net/2012/09/21/mabon-the-feast-of-avalon/.

Struck, Peter T. "Calendar of Greek Religious Festivals — Boedromion." *Greek and Roman Mythology Online Textbook*. http://www.classics.upenn.edu/myth/php/hymns/index.php?page=calendar.

Theoi Project. "RAPE OF PERSEPHONE 1 : Greek Mythology." *Theoi.com*. Accessed June 30, 2014. http://www.theoi.com/Khthonios/HaidesPersephone1.html.

Tiverton Astronomy Society. "Astro-Archaeology at Stonehenge." Accessed June 30, 2014. http://www.tivas.org.uk
/stonehenge/stone_ast.html.

True Blue Bay Resort, Grenada Hotel. "The History Behind
Grenada's Thanksgiving Day." *True Blue Bay Grenada* (blog),
October 25, 2012. http://www.truebluebay.com/blog
/details/the-history-behind-grenadas-thanksgiving-day.

UCSB English Broadside Ballad Archive. "Ballad of John Barleycorn EBBA ID: 20199." *English Broadside Ballad Archive*, 1640.
http://ebba.english.ucsb.edu/ballad/20199/.citation.

Weston, Jessie L. *From Ritual to Romance:* "Chapter IV. Tammuz
and Adonis." Internet Sacred Text Archive, 1920.
http://www.sacred-texts.com/neu/frr/frr07.htm.

Wilson, Lauren. "Thanksgiving in Liberia." *The Daily Meal: All
Things Food and Drink.* May 9, 2013.
http://www.thedailymeal.com/thanksgiving-liberia.

INDEX

About the Author

Diana Rajchel is the author of *Divorcing a Real Witch: For Pagans and the People That Used to Love Them.*

She is also the former executive editor for the *Pagan Newswire Collective*, the network founded by Jason Pitzl-Waters of *The Wild Hunt.* She works as a journalist, author, blogger, and general creative. She identifies as an eclectic Wiccan with more leanings towards Witch than Wiccan.

Diana has contributed to Llewellyn annuals along with occasional submissions to *Circle Magazine, SageWoman, the Beltane Papers* and *Facing North.* Her writing style is notable among Pagan writers because it almost never begins with a description of a walk in the woods. When it does … look for the rolling head. There always seems to be a rolling head after that.

She is a third-degree Wiccan priestess in the Shadowmoon tradition, an American Eclectic Wiccan tradition.

Rajchel is a San Francisco Bay transplant alongside her non-Pagan life partner. She is an urban gardener and enjoys bellydance, Pilates, hypnosis, and shamanic dance.

Other Books by Diana Rajchel
Samhain